# Spiritual
# Intimacy
*with*
# God

# Spiritual
# Intimacy
## *with*
# God

ALICE SMITH

BETHANY HOUSE PUBLISHERS
*Minneapolis, Minnesota*

Published by Bethany House Publishers
11400 Hampshire Avenue South
Bloomington, Minnesota 55438

Bethany House Publishers is a division of
Baker Publishing Group, Grand Rapids, Michigan.

Printed in the United States of America

**Library of Congress Cataloging-in-Publication Data**

Smith, Alice.
    Spiritual intimacy with God : moving joyfully into the deeper life / Alice Smith.
        p.  cm.
    Summary: "Biblical teaching on the intimate relationship God has with Christians and how that relationship develops, what hinders it, and the results of developing intimacy with God"—Provided by publisher.
    ISBN 978-0-7642-0539-2 (hardcover : alk. paper)  1. Spirituality  2. Intimacy (Psychology)—Religious aspects—Christianity.    I. Title.

BV4501.3.S635      2008
248.4—dc22
                                                          2008014287

## ACKNOWLEDGMENTS

Special thanks to my editor, Karen Kaufman, a friend, an incredible storyteller, and a godly woman. She was able to take concepts that were lodged in my heart and help me place them on paper. Karen, you are a real blessing to me and the body of Christ.

I am also grateful to my Wednesday morning prayer group members, who have diligently prayed for me during the writing of this book.

To my heavenly Bridegroom, Jesus Christ. You are the Apple of my eye, the Joy of my heart, and my Best Friend. It is my great pleasure to be your bride.

Books by
# Alice Smith
FROM BETHANY HOUSE PUBLISHERS

*Beyond the Lie*

*Delivering the Captives*

*Spiritual Intimacy With God*

# CONTENTS

Introduction: Deeper Life    11

*1* Intimacy, More Than a Beginning    15

*2* Becoming Real    21

*3* Intimacy Killers    27

*4* Seasons of Intimacy    37

*5* Legacy of Mentors    51

*6* Gifts for Developing Intimacy    61

7 Intimacy and the Practice of Prayer    77

*8* Rewards for Intimacy    91

*9* Intimacy in Action    107

*10* The Oneness of Intimacy    123

*11* Ten Virgins and Two Brides    135

Suggested Reading    145

Notes    149

# Deeper Life

Many years ago, I saw a movie in which a man agreed to climb into a submarine that was minimized to the size of a human cell and then injected into a body. Once inside, he was able to study the way it worked and receive a fresh revelation of the heart. But don't worry. This book is not some crazy science odyssey. Rather, it is a look at intimacy that will take you on a relational journey deep into the heart of God.

I invite you to find a cozy spot where you can curl up and join me as we plumb the depths of the Lord's heart and uncover the things that have hindered us from remaining there. We'll look at our reasons for keeping him at a distance and discover that he *could never*, *would never*, and *has never* forsaken us. Oh sure, people have and circumstances have, but God has not.

I'm reminded of an email I received from Chuck and Delsie Moore, a precious couple who are board members of the U.S. Prayer Center. Chuck is a kind, gentle man who radiates Jesus' love. He's also a general in God's army of prayer warriors. He and his faithful wife Delsie are committed to family, and she cares for their grandchildren in their home. Chuck sent me the following story, and I hope your heart will be as touched by it as mine was. I'll let Chuck tell it in his own words:

*Elly is a shy two-year-old, a very precious little grand-daughter. Delsie cares for Elly while her parents work so I see her most every day, and for some unknown reason, she has been very standoffish with me. For the longest time, whenever I would see her I'd say, "Hi, Elly!" And she would respond in her stern little voice, "NO!" I tried and tried to win her love to no avail. All she ever said was, "NO!"*

*One evening while the family was together, Elly wanted her mother to read a story to her. But her mother was busy preparing supper so I said, "Elly, I will read the book to you." To my surprise she climbed up in my lap and listened intently. Then as soon as I finished, Elly went back to her usual, "NO!"*

*However, little by little over the past few months she has honored me with an occasional "Hi" and sometimes even "Hi, Poppa." Yesterday when I arrived at my son's house, Elly was standing in the driveway. Without hesitation, she ran straight to me and jumped up into my arms. Of course I smothered her with hugs and kisses.*

*Isn't this a picture of our relationship with our heavenly Father? He longs for intimacy with us and draws us to himself time after time, even when we continue to say "NO!" Sometimes, when we want something bad enough, we will come to him, but after we get it we go back to "NO!" And yet he doesn't give up. God loves us, and because he does, he keeps on trying to build a relationship with us.*

*We may even get to the point where we will say, "Hi!"*
*and "Thank you," and think we have a relationship with*
*him. All the while what he really wants is for us to jump*
*into his arms so he can lavish his love on us.*[1]

Friend, that's his invitation to you. No matter how much or little intimacy you have with God right now, he wants to take you deeper. He wants you to jump into his arms so he can lavish his love on you. Come on. Let's make the jump together.

# CHAPTER 1

# Intimacy, More Than a Beginning

Few occasions are as memorable as a wedding. Months and sometimes even years of costly preparation culminate in this one life-changing event. The church is filled with splendor and expectation. Onlookers gather, and ushers hurry to ensure that everyone is seated appropriately, while the bridegroom waits with jubilant anticipation. The guests smile approvingly as the proud groom readies himself to receive the focus of his life's affection. Finally, everyone is poised to gaze upon one person—the bride.

The majestic wedding march begins. All rise. "Here comes the bride. . . ." Adorned in radiant glory, dressed in pure white, she is a living, breathing miracle. Her gorgeous gown flows gracefully as she inches down the aisle toward her groom. She is flawless—her beauty captivating. The groom is mesmerized. Admiring whispers precede her stroll toward the altar where at last she will behold him.

A new covenant—a new beginning! The invited guests listen with delight as the happy couple pledges their love and promises God to honor this commitment forever! "Will you honor, cherish, and obey?" The choice to do so is sealed with a kiss, and that mouth-to-mouth contact is only the beginning of the intimacy they will share in the years and decades to come.

Everyone understands that the ceremony is merely a legal beginning, a public display of commitment. The real bond will be consummated behind closed doors, in the private place where the husband's love is offered without conditions. There, his irresistible devotion to her becomes the impetus for her choice to trust him. Like two glasses of water emptied into the same pitcher, they become one.

## LOVED INTO CHANGE, CHANGED INTO LOVE

When Eddie and I married nearly forty years ago, we could not have been more different. For example, Eddie's siblings (two brothers) weren't exactly huggers and kissers . . . boys! But my family (two sisters and a brother) has always been touchy-feely. In fact, Eddie delights in telling the story of his first meeting with my relatives. The moment we entered the house, they all started hugging and kissing each other on the lips. Poor Eddie. He didn't know what hit him. He was simply stunned by such an outpouring of affection. But you should see Eddie today. What a lover! He hugs, pats on shoulders, and freely kisses our children and grandchildren. He has been changed by love.

And I've been changed too. When we first married, I was so naïve. I believed that everyone's intentions toward us were good. Eddie, on the other hand, was an evangelist with street smarts who could easily discern the wolves in sheep's clothing. By trusting his good sense, I have learned to be wiser in making connections.

Even the way we sing together has changed. We began our ministry in music evangelism, and when I listen to our first album I get a real chuckle. Eddie's voice sounds like a mellow Andy Williams and mine like opera singer Beverly Sills. Two opposite styles! Fortunately, after all these years our two voices have blended beautifully into one.

I remember laughing at a comic who said, "My wife and I were happy for twenty years—then we met and married." Eddie and I can attest to the fact that marriage is work. Neither of us set out to redesign the other, and yet we have both been so changed by the intimacy we share that people now tell us we talk, act, and probably in time will even look alike.

The way of the bride and the bridegroom is analogous to our intimate journey with the Lord Jesus. At salvation, we are wed to him. We say yes to the commitment, but we don't really know what to expect. As we spend time together his love changes us. We become more open and loving toward those around us. We become more like Jesus. And as we realize that nothing can separate us from his love, trust is learned and relearned in the privacy of our hearts. Loss can't separate us, ruin can't, storms can't, betrayal can't—even death can't. That love becomes a firm foundation that we can always count on. Knowing that we can always fall back on God's love gives us the freedom and courage to take risks and do whatever he tells us to do. A love that cannot be taken from us is a love that will eventually foster enough trust to change us.

When God refers to us as the bride—and men he's talking to you too—he means that he is married to the idea of remaking you and me into everything we are capable of being. Saying "I do" to him is saying that you will let him love you into change—and eventually you will be so transformed that others do not recognize the former you.

*In "The Happy Hypocrite" Max Beerbohm tells about a regency rake [a man of habitual immoral conduct] named Lord George Hell, debauched and profligate [given to wild perversion], who falls in love with a saintly girl, and, in order to win her love, covers his bloated features with the mask of a saint. The girl is deceived and becomes his bride, and they live together happily until a wicked lady from Lord George Hell's wicked past turns up to expose him for the scoundrel she knows him to be and challenges him to take off his mask. So sadly, having no choice, he takes it off, and lo and behold beneath the saint's mask is the face of the saint he has become by wearing it in love.[1]*

When the Lord pursues us, weds us, and gives us a place to belong, we can't help but have a new confidence and unending love for him. Our mask comes off, for love that cannot be taken from us will most assuredly change us.

## LOVE IS NOT A "HOW TO"

The most important thing I have learned about God's love is that it is not a "how to" but rather a "belonging to." He has not only sought you out but he has also engraved you on the palms of his hands (Isa. 49:16). You belong to him.

A friend recently told me the story of a man who, while driving his fancy white Cadillac down the highway, opened the door and shoved his collie out onto the pavement. Bloodied and baffled, the dog finally rose on its legs and chased after the master who had cast him aside and abused him.

Like that rejected collie, many of us have had such a need for belonging that we too have chased after masters that sought to destroy us. Perhaps you, just like that collie, have experienced the rebuff or abuse of a parent, sibling, spouse, or friend who should have been there to protect you. If so, you may have a distorted image of God, thinking he can't possibly want to love you. You might even fear being known by him. Maybe you're afraid that if you get close, he'll throw you out of his Kingdom or push you into a painfully intolerable lifestyle.

I have good news! The Lord Jesus is in hot pursuit of you. You may have shut him out, failed him so miserably that no one wants to know your name, or left him in some dry desert of disappointment, but he's not going to let you go. He will chase you down the highways and the byways, into the subways and the sewers, just to let you know he loves you. And then, once Jesus has you, you get to decide how deep your relationship will grow.

We cannot find what we do not seek, and we will not trust what we do not know, so let's pursue his heart together. That's right, you and me. Let's take the risk of being known and loved by the Lord Jesus—let's move joyfully into the place of spiritual intimacy and grow deeper.

CHAPTER 2

# Becoming Real

Years ago, a friend confessed that in twenty-seven years of marriage, her husband had never seen her naked. "How did you manage to have three children with your clothes on?" I asked quite naïvely. She explained that her fear of being rejected due to an imperfect body left her no choice but to dress in the bathroom and make love in the dark.

Sadly, like this dear woman, we too are often afraid to let God see our imperfections, erroneously believing he might reject us. We keep our wounded hearts hidden behind closed doors and refuse to remove our robes of pseudo-righteousness or rejected hopelessness because we think God is blind in the dark.

In his book *Mortal Lessons*, Dr. Richard Selzer provides a touching look at how God deals with our flaws:

> *I stand by the bed where a young woman lies, her face postoperative, her mouth twisted in palsy, clownish. A tiny twig of the facial nerve, the one to the muscles of her mouth, has been severed. She will be thus from now on. The surgeon had followed with religious fervor the curve of*

*her flesh; I promise you that. Nevertheless, to remove the
tumor in her cheek, I had cut the little nerve.*

*Her young husband is in the room. He stands on the
opposite side of the bed, and together they seem to dwell in
the evening lamplight, isolated from me, private. Who are
they, I ask myself, he and this wry-mouth I have made,
who gaze at and touch each other so generously, greedily?
The young woman speaks.*

*"Will my mouth always be like this?" she asks.*

*"Yes," I say, "it will. It is because the nerve was cut."*

*She nods, and is silent. But the young man smiles.*

*"I like it," he says. "It is kind of cute."*

*All at once I* know *who he is. I understand, and I
lower my gaze. One is not bold in an encounter with a god.
Unmindful, he bends to kiss her crooked mouth, and I so
close I can see how he twists his own lips to accommodate to
hers, to show her that their kiss still works.*[1]

No one survives in this fallen world without experiencing
at least one severed nerve. We are all, to some degree, twisted
by life's hurts. But our husband, Jesus, is able to fit his perfect
lips over our flaws and kiss us into wholeness. He sees our ugli-
ness, yet he has promised never to leave us or forsake us (Heb.
13:5).

That is what intimacy is all about. Probably the best defi-
nition would be the one that sounds most like the word: *into me
see.* Intimacy is choosing to let someone peer into your heart and
know the naked truth. It is trusting that the one who looks will
not be repulsed or turn away, but instead give compassion and
hope. Intimacy is letting someone plunge into your heart for
the purpose of kissing you with words everywhere it hurts.

## PERFECT LOVE CASTS OUT FEAR

Nothing robs intimacy as surely as fear. Fear is the thing that often drives us to other lovers, addictions, and such. I know of a young man, brilliant and so gifted, who was gang-raped as a boy. The experience made him feel damaged to the point that he would not let anyone get close, especially God. As he grew, he turned to alcohol to medicate his pain, until one day when he lost his ability to feel. I've often wondered what he could and might become if only he would run to God with his fear, if only he would let the Lord Jesus give him a healing kiss on his wounded heart.

Of course, not everyone drowns their fear of being uncovered in drugs and alcohol. I chose what some might call a respectable cover-up for my past feelings of inadequacy.

In the spring of 1989, God began to captivate my heart and expose a fear so respectably sheathed in activity that I didn't know it was there. As a top-producing real estate agent in northwest Houston, I had a frenzied schedule. I also taught an adult Sunday school class and led a weekly prayer meeting. Busy, busy, busy. Then, Eddie and I attended a Leonard Ravenhill conference. Ravenhill, an old-time no-nonsense preacher, is the author of the classic book *Why Revival Tarries* (Bethany House, 1959; still in print). In it he blasts the world system that has crept into the church and the lack of intimate prayer among Christians.

When Ravenhill preached that day, his words stung like a bee. The Lord had already been speaking to my heart about "letting go," but I didn't fully understand. As I lay on the floor of that large conference center, surrounded by thousands of people, I knew the Holy Spirit was wooing me into a deeper place in my relationship with him.

A few months after the conference, my prayer times became so weepy that I knew God was up to something. I scheduled time for a personal retreat and invited my friend and co-worker Charlene Mundy to join me.

Friday night Charlene read the Bible aloud for a few minutes before we lay facedown on the floor of our hotel room. While Charlene was praying, I lost awareness of both her prayer and her presence.

The supernatural presence of God's Spirit enveloped me until I began weeping deep in my soul. Suddenly, I sensed the Lord speaking. (As of this writing, I have never heard the audible voice of God, nor did I hear it that night, but the Lord spoke clearly within my spirit.) "Alice, let go of your real estate career. Trust me with 1990. Give yourself totally to me and devote yourself to prayer and fasting for one year."

My intense struggle and fear of the unknown left me conflicted because I knew things were about to change forever, and frankly, I liked my life the way it was!

On January 1, 1990 (approximately eight months after the Ravenhill conference), I reticently said good-bye to my profession. I would miss the people, the ability to set my own schedule, and the money that enabled Eddie and me to minister in other nations. I wondered how we would survive financially without that extra income. I wanted a closer walk with Christ, but I wasn't sure he could be trusted to meet our financial needs.

I continued to wrestle with the Lord for hours that night in October 1989 and finally let go of several self-esteem areas, when he asked me to remove all jewelry except for my wedding ring and watch, to refrain from wearing eye shadow or nail polish, to stop any extra maintenance on my hair (yikes! . . . vanity, vanity, all is vanity), and to discontinue professional nail care until the end of the year! Hey, I know what you're thinking! I'm with you! I wanted to *rebuke* the devil, but I recognized God's voice.

That's when the core of my fear was finally exposed. Jesus revealed that my significance was anchored in my appearance, the need to make a good impression on others, and a desire to communicate that I had my act together. The truth is I had a fear of being unlovable—and that fear had prevented me from opening my heart fully to Christ. I was *working* for love rather than *resting* in love, and I was not being myself.

Stripped of outward adornments, I felt vulnerable and naked. Immediately I sensed the expectant embarrassment of having to answer friends and family. I could feel the hook of how important their opinions were to me. With my spiritual eyes now open, I finally saw how I had hidden my true identity behind a façade of cosmetics, jewelry, and career.

What I needed that evening in 1989 was a new and deeper relationship of trust with Jesus, my heavenly Bridegroom and Lover of my soul. Jesus sees beyond our physical needs and sets his gaze on our hearts. My challenge was: *Could I release my need to impress others with my significance?* I continued to remind myself that God feeds faith; the devil feeds fear.

As I left the hotel room I heard the Holy Spirit whisper in my heart, "Alice, my eternal purpose is more important than your temporary pain." With that, I left to face a new season of intimacy.

Do you feel the need to impress others? Is there something keeping you from God? You might never be asked to give up the things required of me, but let me assure you that anything you think you must have, or do, or be, to prove your significance is what will keep you from growing more intimate with the Lord. Jesus loves you, not because of your intelligence, or your sense of humor, or your excellence in running the house or a corporation, or any other thing that comes to your mind. He loves you whether or not you attend church, or teach Sunday school, or witness to the unsaved. He loves you at the core of your being, naked and unadorned, flaws and all.

Jesus, the Christ who came in the flesh for you, loves you for one reason: The heavenly Father gave you to him: "Father, I want those you have given me to be with me where I am" (John 17:24). From eternity past until this moment, the Father has announced, "There she is, Son. She's your bride. Go love and redeem her."

So he did.

CHAPTER 3

# Intimacy Killers

Years ago, Eddie and I had friends who worked in ministry in a large church in our town. This couple had enjoyed the big, expensive wedding with hundreds of adoring guests and a reception that would have made Cinderella jealous. What a perfect pair.

We saw them occasionally throughout the years, and their relationship seemed ideal. She wore the glass slipper without causing a crack, and he worked by her side in ministry. With that said, you can probably imagine how stunned I was the day she came to share a deep, dark secret about their marriage. This dear, hurting woman confided that she and her husband had experienced only one night of physical intimacy during their marriage, the wedding night, and that for twelve years she had suffered in silence.

He wanted the title of husband and the public advantages of marriage, but he also wanted to maintain a secret life that included other lovers. For twelve years, she stayed, yearning for intimacy and living a charade. For twelve years they played the intimacy game, but no one ever won!

Eventually, the inevitable happened. He marched into the house announcing that he had fallen in love with another man and that he was leaving her. She was devastated. Without remorse, without concern, without consideration for all the people who had watched them lead ministry in our large suburban city, he just walked out. Busy they had been; intimates they were not!

## The Unfaithful Bride

I've often thought about that couple and wondered how God must feel when we choose other lovers, forfeiting the true intimacy that only he can provide. The book of Hosea addresses this subject better than I can, so let's have a look.

The Lord chose Hosea, whose name means salvation or deliverance, to become a living parable. Hosea, the first of the minor prophets, so loved God and so appreciated God's love for his unfaithful people that he agreed to marry a harlot named Gomer. Their marriage was to be symbolic of God's sacrificial love for us, even when we refuse it.

Imagine the cost: Hosea takes Gomer to be his bride even though her heart is far from him. Then, after giving birth to three children, she returns to a life of prostitution, moving in with one man after another. Eventually, Gomer is bankrupt and forced to sell herself into slavery. Enter Hosea. Again with unwavering commitment, he rushes off to purchase Gomer's freedom and brings her back home. Hosea continues to pursue her with undeserved and undying love until affection is finally returned and intimacy established. Sounds much like a movie script, doesn't it? But Hosea's commitment to Gomer cannot compare to the Lord's love for his bride, the unfaithful church.

Often we, like Gomer, sell ourselves on the trading block to masters that offer a counterfeit intimacy: lust, success, reputation, material possessions, and more. These things promise peace but furnish emptiness. All the while Jesus, the Prince of Peace, has not only paid the price but is also wooing us, pursuing us, and patiently waiting to take us into his heart to establish true intimacy with us there.

## WORKS, AN INTIMACY KILLER

One thing that prevents intimacy is works. Somehow, many of us have swallowed the lie that our work will earn us more of God's love or provide some position of greatness in the Kingdom. So we climb on the treadmill of doing for God and become too busy to pray, too busy to seek his advice, too busy to know his ways. I'm convinced that Satan does not care if you do a good thing, just so he can keep you from God's best. It's *not* your works that Satan's after—he is after your *intimacy*! Your good works can be part of the enemy's strategy for killing the intimacy God desires to share with you.

## SCARED PRAYERLESS

Another of Satan's effective tactics for killing intimacy is fear. A friend told me a hilarious story about evangelist Jesse Duplantis. On a dark and windy night, Jesse was nearly asleep when ghost-like images began moving violently about the room where he lay. He was paralyzed with fear. With a quivering voice and ten white knuckles, Jesse began rebuking the devil and battling demons. After Jesse's sleepless night, daybreak came too soon—however, with it came major revelation. What appeared to be demons proved to be merely a raincoat hanging on a rack

29

by an open window. He had been fighting all night against a man-made piece of cloth flopping in the wind! When he asked the Lord why he had been allowed to struggle so fiercely, the Lord replied, "Jesse, I haven't laughed that hard in years!"

Of course, God does not laugh at our hardships just to get a chuckle at our expense. But he does want us to know that most things we fear cannot actually kill us—they merely kill our intimacy. Years ago, Zig Ziglar offered an accurate acronym for fear: **F**alse **E**vidence **A**ppearing **R**eal. And no matter how strong we become in the Lord, our enemy will always be presenting us with false evidence.

For example, the Old Testament prophet Elijah was a courageous man. Israel's wicked King Ahab and Queen Jezebel had threatened his life, insisting their pagan god had more power than that of the living God Elijah worshiped. So Elijah challenged King Ahab to a duel of divinities. Ahab sent four hundred and fifty of his best false prophets to Mount Carmel, where the confrontation would ensue. Confident, Elijah dared the false prophets as they spent the day calling on their gods to consume the sacrifice they had built. Nothing. They cut themselves, danced, and even begged their demon god. Still nothing. Elijah teased, accusing their god of taking a trip, or visiting the bathroom.

After a day of defeat, it was Elijah's turn. He began by commanding the altar to be removed and rebuilt. (Note: Our hearts are God's altars. We can't build on the sacrifices of another, nor can we experience another's anointing.) Then, with twelve stones representing the twelve tribes of Israel and symbolic of God's government, the altar was constructed. Elijah carefully sacrificed a bull, laid it on the altar, and called for water—lots of water. Victoriously, Elijah summoned fire from heaven to burn up the sacrifice (see 1 Kings 18). It was a day we would all have been proud to watch.

However, in one tiny little turn of a page, we read another story. Here we find the great and mighty Elijah depleted, depressed, and on the run. Jezebel, the queen whose god he had just proven to be worthless, intimidates him. Listen to this:

*Now Ahab told Jezebel everything Elijah had done and how he had killed all the prophets with the sword. So Jezebel sent a messenger to Elijah to say, "May the gods deal with me, be it ever so severely, if by this time tomorrow I do not make your life like that of one of them." Elijah was afraid and* ran for his life. *When he came to Beersheba in Judah, he left his servant there, while he himself went a day's journey into the desert. He came to a broom tree, sat down under it and prayed that he might die. "I have had enough, Lord," he said. "Take my life; I am no better than my ancestors."*

1 Kings 19:1–4, *emphasis added*

This mighty man of God was now intimidated. Rationally, Elijah knew that Jezebel's gods were powerless, and yet he yielded to fear, false evidence appearing real. None of us are beyond moments of intimidation.

I love the end of this story because it's a picture of intimacy restored. God sought out Elijah and he said,

*"Go out, and stand on the mountain before the Lord." And behold, the Lord passed by, and a great and strong wind tore into the mountains and broke the rocks in pieces before the Lord, but the Lord was not in the wind; and after the wind an earthquake, but the Lord was not in the*

*earthquake; and after the earthquake a fire, but the Lord*
*was not in the fire; and after the fire* a still small voice.
1 Kings 19:11–12 NKJV, *emphasis added*

God was not in the wind, nor the earthquake, nor the fire. He was in the still, small voice. You have to be close and attentive to hear the still, small voice—and God desires closeness. We become intimates when we choose to listen intently.

## DISTRACTED AND DESTROYED

Sir Winston Churchill, Great Britain's former prime minister, described how to be rid of an enemy: "If you want to destroy them, distract them." Certainly, Samson could attest to that truth. His story is found in Judges 16. Perhaps you know about him. Here was a young man with an incredible call of God on his life, but women distracted him. Eventually, one woman became his demise—Delilah. Notice that she didn't burst into his life and announce her ambition to sell him to the Philistines. No, it was just one little distraction after another until he completely forgot his mission.

When the Lord first called me to a life of intimacy, I would shut the door to my prayer closet and without fail, the phone would begin to ring. The phone became a distraction to destroy my closeness with God. With the devil's scheme exposed, I learned to set boundaries around my time in prayer by refusing to be disturbed.

Someone said, "If you want to destroy a man's dream, give him another one." Don't allow distractions to destroy your intimacy or your dreams. When we have intimacy with God, his dream becomes ours, and that's what I want for you.

## SELF-HATRED, SPIRITUAL SUICIDE

So many people I know battle with believing that God has good intentions for them. Consumed with self-hatred, they pick and probe themselves to death, always looking for a reason not to be blessed and not to be loved.

I'm reminded of the story told by Mark Hatfield about James Garfield, lay preacher and principal of his denominational college. In 1880, he was elected president of the United States, but after less than four months in office, he was shot in the back with a revolver. He never lost consciousness. At the hospital the doctor probed his back with his little finger to seek the bullet. He couldn't find it, so he tried a silver-tipped probe. Still he couldn't locate the bullet.

Despite the summer heat of Washington, D.C., medical attendants tried to keep him comfortable, but he was growing very weak. Teams of doctors probed the wound for the bullet to no avail. In desperation Alexander Graham Bell, who was working on a little device called the telephone, was summoned to probe the president's back for that small piece of metal. He came, he sought, he too failed.

President Garfield hung on through July, through August, but in September he finally died—not from the wound but from infection. The repeated probing, which physicians thought would help, eventually killed him.[1]

Similarly, when you or I probe our lives looking for reasons to be disqualified from God's love, our souls become infected with shame, doubt, guilt, and self-hatred. We actually come into agreement with Satan's lie that Jesus' death on the cross was not enough. This lie can force us into isolation, a spiritual suicide that kills our intimacy with God.

Am I talking to you? If so, will you agree with me right now that the probing is over? Let's agree that if Jesus loved you enough to lay down his life for you while you were lost, he loves you enough to understand your faults. Please don't reject what God accepts. You are forgiven.

## UNFORGIVENESS, THE SILENT KILLER

Matthew 18 tells the story of a king who was busy auditing his finances. While rustling through his papers, he discovers, much to his chagrin, that one of his servants has borrowed millions of dollars and has not attempted to repay the debt. When the king summons the servant, he sees that the man is incapable of repaying such an enormous sum of money. The king is furious and gives orders to sell the servant, his family, and all of his possessions to pay off the loan. Yikes! Dropping to the floor, the servant begs the king for mercy. And believe it or not, the king grants him a full pardon! That's right . . . zero, zip, nothing! His debt is completely wiped out.

Sadly, the forgiven servant leaves the palace and searches out a man who owes him a few dollars. He grabs the man by the shirt and threatens his life, demanding instant repayment of the loan. But there is no money. Begging for mercy, the man asks for a little more time. But the merciless servant calls the cops and has the man hauled away. "He will be jailed until he can pay every single dollar," he demands.

Some of the other servants have witnessed the incident and run to tell the king. I like the way Jesus unwraps the rest of the story in the *New International Version*:

*Then the master called the servant in. "You wicked servant," he said, "I canceled all that debt of yours because you begged me to. Shouldn't you have had mercy on your fellow servant just as I had on you?" In anger his master turned*

34

*him over to the jailers to be tortured, until he should pay*
*back all he owed. This is how my heavenly Father will*
*treat each of you unless you forgive your brother from your*
*heart.*

Matthew 18:32–35

Yes, you read that right. If we refuse to forgive from the heart, Jesus said we will be turned over to tormentors. Now for me, there could be no greater torture than to know I have lost intimacy with God—lost peace of mind and the deep joy that comes from my relationship with him. I'm sure you feel that way too.

Unforgiveness opens the door to all kinds of torment: disease, addictions, rage, isolation, bitterness, and more. I have even noted that when unforgiveness is present, the most powerful faith healers on this planet cannot remove the problem until the heart is first emptied of all bitterness.

My friend Elizabeth Alves is a great storyteller. In her book *Becoming a Prayer Warrior*, Beth shares about a time when her four-year-old daughter misbehaved at the dinner table in front of guests. Peggy was escorted to her room and told she could not come out until she was sorry.

A few minutes later the door opened, but Peggy remained in her room. Time passed . . . still no Peggy. Finally her daddy, Floyd, went in and sat on the bed beside her. "Peggy," he asked, "are you sorry enough to come out now?"

Peggy crossed her arms tightly across her chest and replied, "Nope! I'm only sorry enough to have the door open."[2]

Sometimes, just like little Peggy, we only want to forgive enough to keep the door open, but we lose our ability to experience intimacy when we don't forgive with a whole heart.

Let me give you something to think about the next time you struggle with getting close to the Lord: "You have captured the heart of God. He cannot bear to live without you. God's dream is to make you right with Him. And the path to the cross tells exactly how far God will go to call you back."[3]

In Mozart's *Requiem*, there is a line that speaks to the heart of each one of us, "Remember, merciful Jesus, that I am the cause of your journey." He remembers. He remembers you.

# CHAPTER 4

# Seasons of Intimacy

You might have heard the story about the man who said, "My wife treats me like a Greek god—she serves me burnt offerings every morning!" Sounds like the first time I prepared a meal for Eddie. Let me begin by explaining that Eddie cooked for the naval officers during part of his military stint—and my man can really cook! I, on the other hand, am the youngest of a large family, so I left the cooking to my older sisters.

Now that you understand our backgrounds, perhaps you will be able to sympathize with my story. As newlyweds we were low on funds, so one night I decided to make pinto beans for dinner. I put a large pot of water on the stove and poured in the full bag of beans—even wondering if there would be enough. Before long, I had one pot, then two pots, and finally three full pots of those obnoxious little devils. Who knew that one bag of anything could multiply so much? You would have thought I was feeding the five thousand! *And*, I wondered, *why would anyone salt a meal before it's cooked?* So I decided to wait and add it later. Those tiny red babies were as tasteless as dirt; some were hard as rocks, others soft as mush.

My dear sweetheart walked in and simply stared at the mess. Graciously, he ate the tasteless beans and suggested that perhaps the physical effects of beans might be something we should save for old age! It was no surprise when I opened my first Christmas gift from Eddie. You guessed it—a cookbook.

Why do I tell you that story? Because I think you can relate. In the early days of our relationships, we are so excited about becoming one and enamored with this new love that we are anxious and willing to make some changes to get along. Those first few weeks and months of marriage are almost enchanting, filled with giddy moments and lots of loving surprises. It's a God-ordained season of getting to know each other.

## Intimacy Requires a Foundation

God is so adamant about laying a foundation for intimacy that he said in Deuteronomy 24:5, "If a man has recently married, he must not be sent to war or have any other duty laid on him. For one year he is to be free to stay at home and bring happiness to the wife he has married." Notice that the husband's duty for the first year of marriage is simply to make his bride happy.

Most of us are attracted to friends and lovers by the joy we expect to receive from them. But our intimate relationships involve those who not only bring us joy, but also help us weather our storms, bear our burdens, and survive the tests of time.

Relationships, whether with God or his people, cycle through seasons. Ecclesiastes 3:1–8 says,

*There is a time for everything, and a season for every activity under heaven: a time to be born and a time to die, a time to plant and a time to uproot, a time to kill and a time to heal, a time to tear down and a time to build, a*

*time to weep and a time to laugh, a time to mourn and a*
*time to dance, a time to scatter stones and a time to gather*
*them, a time to embrace and a time to refrain, a time to*
*search and a time to give up, a time to keep and a time to*
*throw away, a time to tear and a time to mend, a time to*
*be silent and a time to speak, a time to love and a time to*
*hate, a time for war and a time for peace.*

I'm convinced that these eight verses provide a foretaste of the seasons we must walk through with our heavenly Bridegroom in order to truly know his heart, in order to become intimates.

## SEASONS OF DISCLOSURE

Don't you just love springtime? It's that time of year when every living thing seems to be alive with song and the world is suddenly awakened to joy. The warm breath of spring thaws the frozen lakes and blows across the fields until the flowers open their sleepy petals. Everything feels fresh and full of life.

Spring seasons in our relationship with God are those "first love" periods when the Lord is actively disclosing himself, and we just can't get enough time alone with him. We feel his closeness, and there is almost a tangible presence in it. During these seasons, life is abuzz with fresh words from the Lord, new revelation, and rich times of seeing him kiss our lives with unexpected blessings.

It's as if we have just awakened to love. We want to gorge ourselves with more and more of his Word. Our conversations with him are lively, and even the simplest prayers seem to receive answers. Yes, these are seasons of disclosure. We tell him every detail about ourselves (as if he didn't know) and share our hopes and dreams with him. The fragrance of our prayers is sweet and lingers in the atmosphere we carry. We feel known and loved and want to share that love with the whole world.

Spring is a planting time and everything is in seed form, but each new season of disclosure will require a new process of trust and maturity. Seeds need water and time to grow strong and produce fruit. After decades of walking with the Lord, I assure you that many of the prophetic words I received in my seasons of disclosure made my heart leap with joy. What I did not know is that they would take years to come to pass and that those words would go through many seasons before they would finally burst into the reality of my life.

Are you in a season of disclosure? If so, know that the prophetic words and new revelations you are receiving may take time to become a reality. Permit me to explain.

On June 27, 1985, I had a powerful encounter with God. I had just become a new mom. My sole ambition at that time was to mother our new baby and stay intimate with the Lord. Eddie and I had started a new church so I was also teaching Sunday school. I thought my life was as full as it would ever be.

The Lord, however, had other plans. That day in my prayer closet, the Lord gave me a prophetic word from Isaiah 55:3–5, in which he said,

*Give ear and come to me; hear me, that your soul may live. I will make an everlasting covenant with you, my faithful love promised to David. See, I have made him a witness to the peoples, a leader and commander of the peoples. Surely you will summon nations you know not, and nations that do not know you will hasten to you, because of the Lord your God, the Holy One of Israel, for he has endowed you with splendor.*

I sobbed, thinking that God wanted to make a covenant with me and that he loved me even as he had loved David. When he told me he was calling me to be a leader and that I would change nations, I thought, *The only thing I'm changing is diapers, Lord! How can this be?* But I also knew that if God gave that word, and he did, he would bring it to pass in his way and in his time.

Remember, I received that word in 1985, during a season of disclosure. But, it wasn't until September of 1996 that I spoke at my first national meeting and started ministering to the nations. I felt so unqualified and so nervous before that first conference that I chose to wear my longest skirt so people wouldn't see my legs shaking! Today, I travel internationally, teaching the body of Christ about the history of their nations and how to pray for change.

Another component God used to fulfill his word to me is the publication of *Beyond the Veil*. The book was rejected fourteen times when I finally decided to self-publish. Shortly thereafter, Kyle Duncan (at that time from Regal Books) attended one of my conferences and sought me out, even though his company had turned down the book twice before. Regal finally published the bestselling book, and it has been translated into eight other languages to date. Dear friend, if the Lord tells you that he is going to do something in you, or through you, believe it— because nothing is impossible with God!

I'd like to stop right here and share an important key that the Lord taught me about seasons of disclosure. When you receive a word, hold it in your heart and do not share it unless God tells you to do so. Secrets must be held until they are ready to be fulfilled. Psalm 25:14 says, "The Lord confides in those who fear him; he makes his covenant known to them." One detriment to sharing with others is that some people cannot visualize you the way God sees you. They may dash your dreams and drive you

41

into a spirit of unbelief, which can become a stronghold. So just trust God to bring you forward when the timing is right.

And by the way, if God gives you a promise, let him take the lead in fulfilling it. Many Christians have run ahead of God and made a mess that took years to clean up. When we take the reins from the Lord, pride runs away with us and we end up losing direction. Jeremiah 29:11 says that God knows the plans he has for you—and he knows how to get you there. Your fulfillment will probably come in a season when you least expect it.

## SEASONS OF PASSION

Just as summer follows spring, seasons of passion follow seasons of disclosure. We've heard that God wants to use us, and now our fervor for action begins to intensify. The presence of the Lord is with us, and we feel empowered by his favor and his answers to our prayers. Things begin to heat up during this time, especially our zeal.

Often Christians in a season of passion think they have all the answers and that they can conquer the world for the Lord. We seem to easily attain breakthroughs and feel undefeatable. Consider Moses. Early in his life, in a season of passion, Moses sought to help God by killing an Egyptian with his bare hands. But later in a season of disclosure, God revealed to Moses that he would deliver his people from the Egyptians. He knew God wanted to use him, and he believed himself to be more than fit for the task.

In a season of passion, prayer is fun and we feel powerful. We are ready to take on the devil, until we find that "the devil in the mirror" is our own independent spirit. Part of our independence comes from seeing the power of our spiritual gifts at work and the favor of God resting on us. The temptation is to transfer our reliance from *the Lord of the work* to *the work of the Lord.* When that happens, humility is insidiously replaced by pride.

I've seen some exceptionally gifted Christians snagged by the lure of stardom during a season of passion. Before long they are being dragged about by their gifts, and instead of being hooked on Jesus, they are hooked on their own celebrity status. A prima donna attitude ensues with staggering demands. Next, a spirit of mammon takes over—mammon is money without a Kingdom mission. The mission now is to obtain larger homes, bigger cars, private jets, and privileged living. When passions turn from God to self, moral failure often becomes inevitable. Of course, many people who have all the benefits of financial prosperity in ministry have remained faithful and kept their focus on God. Praise the Lord for ministries that impact millions.

Today, Jim Bakker is the real deal, humble and sold out to God. But I'll never forget that heartbreaking day when Jim, a weeping and broken man, was handcuffed and led off to prison. I cried too. Jim had started fervently with a mission to serve God, but he was seduced by mammon during a season of passion. We must all guard ourselves when passions are accelerated. Without the Lord's help, any of us can fall to some degree for self-promotion, as our brother Jim did, because Satan is always looking for a way to rob us of God's favor.

I don't mean to alarm you. Seasons of passion are needed and should be appreciated. They spur us on to learn more of God's ways, especially when we are surrounded with the right mentors. One person who changed my life during a season of passion was Corrie ten Boom, a Dutch Christian who was arrested and sent to a Nazi concentration camp for hiding Jews and helping them to escape during the 1940s.

Eddie and I were privileged to spend an evening with Miss Ten Boom at a dinner party back in the early '70s. Those several hours in her presence will forever be among my most cherished memories. On that cold winter night, a small group of us sat by the fire and just listened as Corrie talked about the deeper things of God. Her eyes danced with joy as she spoke to us. Then, lifting her head heavenward, she would talk to the Father in her sweet Dutch accent, "Oh, Father, help your children understand these things." When Eddie and I left the party that night, I understood. I also had a new obsession to experience Jesus with that same kind of intimacy. Little did I know that deeper intimacy would require another season—fall, a season of stripping.

## SEASONS OF STRIPPING

Seasons of stripping, like the fall season, make their entrance so unremarkably that we hardly notice their arrival. Still experiencing success, we don't want to change our stride. We've finally acquired some confidence, some wisdom, and some maturity. The works planted in spring are now robust and ready to be harvested, but we forget that harvesting means stripping the vines until they are barren.

Most of us enter times of stripping satisfied from the past harvests our works have produced. Suddenly, a distinct shift occurs in our ability to make things jive. Sifting through the rubble of our works to find another task to complete for God results in disappointment. We struggle to find satisfaction in past accomplishments and who we once were, but the way is not there.

When the winnowing begins, the very things we counted on vanish before our eyes. I've watched people in seasons of stripping lose their children to drugs, divorce after years of a stable marriage, file for bankruptcy, and face hardships with insurmountable pain. Friendships are prone to fall by the way-

44

side, or even die, because all idols must be brought down. We experience betrayal and wonder, *Where is God?*

In my case, I was caught off guard when a friend I greatly admired suddenly became jealous and tried to destroy my reputation and ministry. After repeatedly trying to amend and reconcile, to no avail, all I could do was walk away from the relationship and pray that God would be my defender. I felt sad and misused. Perhaps you can relate.

During these times, the harder we try to rectify what won't work, the more we realize just how powerless we really are. It seems nobody has a word of guidance, and there is no way to make a connection back to our season of passion. All doors are closing, and like Job, our friends become our misinformed critics.

Just about everyone offers some sort of advice, and the common recommendation is "Seek inner healing." But inner healing is not God's remedy. God doesn't want you rectified or remedied by man. His prescription is John 12:24: "Unless a kernel of wheat falls to the ground and dies. . . ."

If you are in a stripping season, please know that God hasn't discarded you; he merely wants to take you deeper in him. He loves you, dear one. He loves you right where you are in your struggle.

Seasons of stripping echo times of pruning, especially in purpose. I've been told that trees that haven't been cut back will eventually produce bitter fruit. And because God wants you to become better rather than bitter, everything that can be cut off will be cut off, not to harm but to bless and to sweeten your future.

Science makes clear that during fall, as the nights get longer, the glucose (sugar) in the leaves is first sent to the branches and then back down to the roots to preserve the tree. Likewise, our days feel more like nights, and God is now directing our hunger toward things that will root us firmly in him. He will do so through a process so that the experience does not break us, but will instead heal our brokenness by killing the things that separate us from a deeper intimacy with Jesus. Our season of stripping is merely preparation for death in the silence of winter to come.

## SEASONS OF CAVE DWELLING

Winter kills! Surface things, selfish things, must die; only the root endures. Life goes underground. Even the animals go into hiding. The sounds of silence pierce the atmosphere with cruel isolation. Living waters turn to icy lakes. Everything is dammed up: halted. Winter is like heart surgery without anesthesia.

We don't choose winter, but we do choose what we will become as a result of it. Some people choose to become snow-birds and leave behind the relationships and connections that are deepened by winter's trials. That choice, however, results in intimacy lost. Those who choose to endure and stay will be changed; they will become God's intimates.

The Bible records with graphic detail a vivid winter in the life of David. He had been through the season of disclosure as a youth when Samuel anointed him to be king. Then in summer, his season of passion, David slew Goliath; and one would assume he had finally arrived as a mighty man of God, ready to be used for the Kingdom. Of course, fall brought with it a season of stripping in which David was driven away from the palace, was betrayed by his son Absalom, and suffered the death of his friend Jonathan. Fumbling to find a place of belonging, David finally settled in a cave. It was a winter in his life.

By winter's end, we have become a shell of our former selves. No longer can we pretend to be what we are not. Winter forces us to become authentic at the root. We are prone to weeping and sometimes don't know why. Well-meaning people want to "pray off" of us a spirit of grief, or even death. But like David, the weeping king, we must endure life in the cave in order to move into the palace when God finally ushers us into our next spring.

In the cave, David did not connect with the "I've got it all together" crowd that he had encountered in Saul's court. No, he hooked up with other cave dwellers, rejects, unknowns who understood loyalty, character, and the agony of defeat. It was in the cave that David exchanged ambition for submission, triumph for tears, and safety for true character.

Any cave dweller knows that God withdraws his presence to teach us to be still. For example, back in the early '70s I went through a long season of God's silence. It was a time of wounding upon wounding, and I was simply going through the motions. I still have strong memories of an occasion when Eddie and I were in Memphis, Tennessee, for revival meetings, and I had just experienced the agony of a miscarriage. I was trying to hide my devastation and minister to others despite my pain.

One particular night, I wore a lovely long cream dress to the service when a lady who thought I had it all together approached Eddie with an angry, jealous attitude. The woman passionately complained to him that she would give *everything* she had to be like me. She had no way of knowing that I had just lost a baby and that we had lost all our possessions the year before. Eddie replied, "Well, it has cost Alice *everything* to be who she is today."

Ironically, by that time I had felt like an empty shell for almost a year, and yet I was being judged for my outward appearance. That's winter! That's life in the cave! People outside have no idea what we are going through, because it's going on at the root level.

Warning: Self-pity in the cave can drive us toward false dependencies such as psychologists, pills, pessimism, and depression. My advice: Stand still and see the salvation of the Lord! He promised never to leave you or forsake you, and he never will. Allow Jesus to change you during the winter of your life!

## SEASONED RESULTS

The seasons of intimacy are God's way of teaching us that it's no longer about us trying to be in Christ; it's about Christ in us, the hope of glory. They also teach us to live with our hands open so that God can remove certain things and add others without a flinch in our souls.

I'm reminded of the story of Horatio G. Spafford, who wrote the song "It Is Well With My Soul," originally titled "Peace Attends My Way."

Horatio, a successful businessman, and his family were Presbyterians who lost all their worldly possessions in the 1871 Chicago fire. Then in the fall of 1873, business obligations prevented Horatio from joining his wife and four daughters when they set sail on the *Ville du Havre* to vacation in Europe. As the mighty ocean liner charted its course through the icy waters of the Atlantic Ocean, it was struck by an English ship and sunk within twelve minutes. Mrs. Spafford was among the survivors, but all four girls were lost in the wreckage of that perilous event.

Sometime later Horatio was crossing the Atlantic on his way to England when the ship's captain summoned him to the bridge. The captain pointed to the place where his four daughters had lost their lives. Mr. Spafford, flowing in the supernatural peace and comfort of the Holy Spirit, penned the following words:

*When peace, like a river, attendeth my way,*
*When sorrows like sea billows roll;*
*Whatever my lot, Thou has taught me to say,*
*"It is well, it is well with my soul."*[1]

No matter what season you are in right now, please know that there is a reason for the season and a lesson in the season that will teach you to say, "It is well, it is well with my soul." Now that's intimacy!

# CHAPTER 5

# Legacy of Mentors

*It was undoubtedly the most intriguing article I had read in a long time.*

*Evidently, Elvis Presley was making another comeback. A few years ago, a Presley look-alike contest took place in New England and the* Boston Globe *was there to cover it. They ran a story which spotlighted a disillusioned fan named Dennis Wise. His comments are revealing:*

*"Elvis Presley was and is my idol. I've seen his concerts, I have every album he's recorded, and watched every movie he's made. I once got a hair contour like his, and now I have a face-lift that looks just like him. . . . I have won Elvis look-alike contests dozens of times. . . . I have ticket stubs and clippings from programs around the world; I even own some Elvis pillows from Japan.*

*"I wanted him to see me, so I would often storm the stage, during and after the concerts. . . . I don't think he ever noticed me. I once even climbed the walls around*

*Graceland, the Presley mansion, to catch a glimpse of him. I think it might have been him wandering through the house as I looked through my binoculars, but I'm not sure. What an irony. It's actually funny. All the effort I put into following him . . . and I never could seem to get close."*

*Do you hear the despondency in his words? Here's a fan who began following Elvis with high expectations and ended with low fulfillment. You might call it raw disappointment. The words are haunting: "I don't think he ever noticed me. . . . I never could seem to get close."*

*Hmmm. After reading this, I immediately thought about my relationship with God. I wonder how many times I've felt this way about God, over the years—much less been bold enough to admit it. And, I am a leader! I've led Bible studies, prayed, preached, fasted, sang the songs and even lifted my hands to Him. Yet, if I'd get honest about it, at times I've felt the same way Dennis Wise felt about his idol, Elvis: "All the effort I put into following Him . . . and I never could seem to get close."[1]*

Perhaps you too have shared Dennis's frustration—times when intimacy with God seemed unattainable. Whether we admit it or not, every person in pursuit of God has struggled to feel his presence. Having taught throughout the world about intimacy with God, some people assume I have an advantage over them. I don't. I must cultivate, maintain, and guard my intimacy with the Lord . . . just like you.

We can learn about cultivating intimacy by studying the Bible and the legacy biblical mentors have left us. Often Scripture reveals the story of prideful, self-assured individuals who through the process of ongoing revelation by God are forever changed to become his close intimates. It's been said that life must be lived with foresight, but it can only be understood with hindsight. Let's spend a few pages reviewing the lives of some intimates and see what we can learn from them.

## MOSES, A LEGACY OF SURRENDER

Moses had the benefit of being raised in an Egyptian palace. He had learned the ways of royalty and received the respect, position, and privilege that only nobility can provide. But when God's finger pointed in his direction, Moses was driven off into the wilderness to become alone and abased.

Everything he had learned in terms of Pharaoh's world had to be laid down and unlearned so he could walk in God's kind of nobility—servant leadership. And what greater place to learn the ways of God than in the wilderness! There, he had no distractions. There, he met the Lord in the burning bush and came to know his voice. There, he learned to take his shoes off and walk in humility. There, he learned his purpose and how to follow God.

Moses learned during his forty-year wilderness that his wounds were needed in order to identify with the hearts and hurts of those he would lead. Dear friend, please don't waste your dry periods, because they are your credentials for helping others along the way.

Can you imagine being asked to lead a nation through a wilderness? Moses was nervous. Who wouldn't be! He knew that if God didn't show up, he didn't want to be there either. Let's listen in on the conversation between Moses and God: " 'If it is true that you look favorably on me, let me know your ways so I may understand you more fully and continue to enjoy your favor. And remember that this nation is your very own people.'

The Lord replied, 'I will personally go with you, Moses, and I will give you rest—everything will be fine for you.' Then Moses said, 'If you don't personally go with us, don't make us leave this place' " (Ex. 33:13–15 NLT).

Moses would not go forward without the presence of the Lord. He had a reluctance to act until he knew what the outcome would be, but God merely assured Moses of his presence and ability to guide his steps. You too may be afraid to move forward. Questions invade your mind: *Did God really tell me to do this? What happens if I fail?*

I'm reminded of a time when a man asked Mother Teresa to pray for guidance for his future. Her reply, "Why should you have a road map when the rest of us have to walk by faith?"

Part of developing intimacy is walking with God through our dilemmas and letting him be our support. During crises, I have often felt painfully disturbed, distracted, and unsure. I wondered how I could possibly accomplish what God called me to do because I was so unprepared for the task. Moses didn't feel prepared to face his crisis in leading the nation either, yet God told him, "As my glorious presence passes by, I will hide you in the crevice of the rock and cover you with my hand until I have passed by. Then I will remove my hand and let you see me from behind. But my face will not be seen" (Ex. 33:22–23 NLT).

Sometimes we don't know what God is doing until we see it in hindsight. It is then that we know that he was there all the time, and we feel more willing to trust him again. This is exactly how the Lord develops us, and the result is greater intimacy.

I once heard about a farmer who approached his milking cow carrying a bucket. He stopped and asked, "Okay, Molly, what's it going to be today—milk or chopped steak?" I know that example might sound silly, but people often get the idea that if they pursue the Lord and begin to go deeper with him, the cost will be more than they are willing to pay. We all long for more of his presence, but then we read verses such as Luke 12:48, which tells us that "from everyone who has been given much, much will be demanded; and from the one who has been entrusted with much, much more will be asked."

God wrote these words in the Bible to encourage us. This verse means that the more we receive and prove ourselves trustworthy, the more we will be trusted to do greater things. But Satan twists the way we perceive the motivation of God's heart so that we fear being disqualified if we blow it. The resulting fear leads to paralysis.

Have you worried that if you disobeyed or did something stupid during the crunch time, you would be disqualified for future ministry opportunities? If so, you've believed a lie. Relax. The Lord is good. He will never leave you in a defeated place. He simply wants us to stay humble, teachable, and always hungry for more of him. Jesus is a marvelous guide.

The cost of intimacy is great, but living without it is far more costly! Exodus 33:11 records that God called Moses his friend, and friends have advantages. Imagine the joy of hearing the Father call you friend too!

## DAVID, A LEGACY OF TRUST

One great advantage of friendship is knowing you have someone to confide in, someone to run to in times of trouble, someone who will love you no matter how miserably you have messed up. David ran to the Lord in every crisis of his life because he believed that God loved him. He also believed that God would listen and not judge him for his feelings. David did not pretend. He emptied all his fears before the Lord: "In my distress I called upon the Lord, and cried to my God: and he did hear my voice out of his temple, and my cry did enter into his ears. . . . He delivered me" (2 Sam. 22:7, 18 KJV). Do you hear the honesty? Do you hear the trust?

David so longed for closeness with the Lord that he would compose songs telling of his great love. I'm reminded of a quote by Martin Luther in which he said, "He who worships, prays twice." David enjoyed a double portion of intimacy because his whole life was lived in front of God as worship.

Even after he sinned with Bathsheba, David ran to God with the consequences, transparent and repentant. Friend, that's how intimacy is cultivated. The devil would have us believe that we should hide our faults in fear of God's rejection, but the Lord wants us to run to him with our messes. He wants to be our hiding place, our protector, the one who will hear the worst in us and still draw out the best. He wants to be the shelter we run to in the storm.

No matter how fiercely the storms blow, we determine where they will take us by choosing the direction of our trust. David let his storms take him further and further into intimacy. When he was between a rock and a hard place, he let God be his rock: "The Lord is my rock, my fortress and my deliverer; my God is my rock, in whom I take refuge, my shield and the horn of my salvation. He is my *stronghold*, my refuge and my savior—from violent men you save me. I call to the Lord, who is worthy of praise, and I am saved from my enemies" (2 Sam. 22:2–4, italics added).

Who is your rock? Where do you run when the enemies of shame, hurt, betrayal, and the like are pursuing you? David had the answer: Call on God.

Did you catch the word *stronghold*? We can either choose to run to counterfeit forms of love such as pills, alcohol, food, shopping, pornography, and more and allow those things to have a *strong hold* on us, or we can run to God and allow him to have a *strong hold* on our lives. Satan will use the circumstance to imprison us until we feel like inmates. Oh but God, he will take us deeper and turn us into spiritual intimates. That's when the storm becomes the advantage!

## JOHN, A LEGACY OF LOVE

Can you imagine being known as the disciple whom Jesus loved? John was the only disciple to bear this title; he was Jesus' best friend. Like your best friend and mine, John was there for Jesus at the most important times of his life. He sat with his head buried in Jesus' chest during the Last Supper, and was so concerned about being the one who would betray him that he asked, "Is it I?" It was John whom Jesus entrusted with the care of his mother while dying on the cross. It was John who was first at the tomb after Jesus' resurrection. It was John who first recognized Jesus standing on the shore in Galilee.

John was consumed with Jesus all the days of his life. He was plunged into boiling oil and then exiled—all because he loved his Lord. In the popular book *Hinds' Feet on High Places*, the main character, Much-Afraid, tells the Shepherd that she wants to learn about love. He then stretches out his hand. In his palm is a long, sharp thorn. He goes on to explain that if she wants to know how to love, she must allow him to place that thorn in her heart:

> *"The [thorn] looks very sharp," she said shrinkingly.*
> *"Won't it hurt if you put it into my heart?" He answered*
> *gently, "It is so sharp that it slips in very quickly. But,*
> *Much-Afraid, I have already warned you that Love and*

*Pain go together, for a time at least. If you would know
Love, you must know pain too."*[2]

From the hindsight of John's biography, we have the advantage of discovering that intimacy will always cost us something.
John suffered greatly to know the Lord, but he also left us
with the book of Revelation, a picture of God's heart and all
that is to come. No one has ever received more revelation
than John.

Intimates of Jesus are those who count the cost and take
the thorn in the heart anyway.

## PAUL, A LEGACY OF COMMITMENT

I often tell people that when I die, I want to see Jesus, my
parents, my sister, Eddie's parents—and the feisty, probably
short like me (his name means "little"), intense apostle named
Paul. This guy can easily be described as an "in your face" kind
of disciple. He was so headstrong that Jesus had to unceremo-
niously dismount him from his horse in Damascus to get his
attention. Perhaps it is Paul who gave us the phrase "God will
knock you off your high horse!" (Pun intended!)

Before his conversion, Paul (formerly Saul) was a prideful
Roman zealot who persecuted the church. Then, in Acts 9:4,
the Lord Jesus appears to him and asks, "Saul, Saul, why do you
persecute me?" Saul had believed he was doing God a favor—
that is, until he met God's Son. One divine encounter with
Jesus drove his whole life from that time on, and the persecutor
became the persecuted for Christ's sake. The converted Paul
answered Christ's initial question by becoming a living truth:
We do not love a God we cannot see until we see the face of
God in everyone we meet.

Paul understood the price that Jesus paid for his life. He lived out the truth that he who is forgiven much loves much, and that truth became the catalyst for intimacy. Paul was shipwrecked, rejected, publicly beaten, imprisoned, and relentlessly pursued by the Pharisees, yet he counted all his suffering as "rubbish" (Phil. 3:8) in comparison to his gain in Christ.

Paul knew the meaning of commitment; he knew it because he understood the cost Jesus had paid for his life, for your life, and for the lives of all believers to come. Having been arrested by love, he devoted his life to loving others. He loved what God loved—people—and he would pay any price to win them for the Lord. Paul understood what it meant to lay down his life for others, and that kind of surrender brought an intimacy that few others have ever known.

It would be easy to look at Paul's example and feel hopeless in comparison. But Paul was the least likely candidate for intimacy. He began as a murderer, with a reputation for being hard and cruel. And I believe God showed us his past to give you and me hope for the future. When we fully grasp God's love for the world, we cannot help but love it too.

Who can forget the impact of a wealthy young man who surrendered everything to embrace a life of poverty for Christ's sake! That man was Saint Francis of Assisi. You have probably read his famous prayer. Now let God use it to draw you deeper into his heart.

*Lord, make me an instrument of your peace.*
*Where there is hatred, let me sow love;*
*where there is injury, pardon;*
*where there is doubt, faith;*
*where there is despair, hope;*
*where there is darkness, light;*
*where there is sadness, joy.*

*O Divine Master, grant that I may not so much seek to be
consoled as to console,
to be understood as to understand;
to be loved as to love.
For it is in giving that we receive;
it is in pardoning that we are pardoned;
and it is in dying that we are born to eternal life.*

As we grow deeper in intimacy, we too will embrace the characteristics of biblical mentors and bring life to people who are dying without the Lord.

A great fable sometimes holds a great truth. For example, "the story of the Empress Helena tells how she went to the Holy Land to find the Cross. Excavations were made, and three crosses were found; but how were they to know which was the true one? So they took a corpse and put it upon one and another; and, as soon as the corpse touched the Savior's Cross, it started to live. Now, you are demonstrating the divinity of Christianity, and that is how you test it—the Cross makes these dead men live."[3]

When the cross impacts us with true intimacy, no doubt others will see our closeness with Jesus Christ and want that same kind of intimacy themselves.

# CHAPTER 6

# Gifts for Developing Intimacy

*Chippie the parakeet never saw it coming. One second he was peacefully perched in his cage. The next he was sucked in, washed up, and blown over.*

*The problems began when Chippie's owner decided to clean Chippie's cage with a vacuum cleaner. She removed the attachment from the end of the hose and stuck it in the cage. The phone rang, and she turned to pick it up. She'd barely said "hello" when "sssopp!" Chippie got sucked in.*

*The bird owner gasped, put down the phone, turned off the vacuum, and opened the bag. There was Chippie—still alive, but stunned.*

*Since the bird was covered with dust and soot, she grabbed him and raced to the bathroom, turned on the faucet, and held Chippie under the running water. Then, realizing that Chippie was soaked and shivering, she did what any compassionate bird owner would do . . . she reached for the hair dryer and blasted the pet with hot air.*

*Poor Chippie never knew what hit him.*

> *A few days after the trauma, the reporter who'd ini-*
> *tially written about the event contacted Chippie's owner to*
> *see how the bird was recovering. "Well," she replied, "Chip-*
> *pie doesn't sing much anymore—he just sits and stares."*
>
> *It's hard not to see why. Sucked in, washed up, and*
> *blown over . . . that's enough to steal the song from the*
> *stoutest heart.*[1]

Sometimes we, just like Chippie, feel as though we've been sucked up and spit out by life, and God seems very far away. We need him more than ever, but we don't know how to establish intimacy. It's during those times that we can turn to Jesus and rely on his gifts to put a song back in our hearts.

## THE GIFT OF THE HOLY SPIRIT

Jesus' last words before he died were, "It is finished" (John 19:30). It is his nature to finish what he starts. He never has and never will leave you or me without a way to finish the work he began in us. He even promises that "God, who began the good work within you, will continue his work until it is finally finished on the day when Christ Jesus returns" (Phil. 1:6 NLT). Jesus cares that you and I also finish, and finish strong, before we die.

He cares about the details of our lives. Jesus was so concerned for the welfare of others that while he hung on the cross, he entrusted John with the care of his mother so that neither would suffer alone. He was so concerned about your welfare and mine that he left the Comforter, the ever-present Holy Spirit so that you and I would never be alone either. The person of the Holy Spirit comes to live in our hearts, or indwells us (1 Cor. 6:19), to teach us the character of God and to help us eliminate those things that block our intimacy with Jesus.

The Holy Spirit is not a chatterbox. He is soft-spoken and tender, but nonetheless a teacher and counselor for those who *choose* to listen. Some Christians define the Holy Spirit as our conscience, while others refer to him as the umpire of our hearts. I've heard some call him a gut instinct and others call him a God instinct. Regardless of how we describe him, most Christians struggle to discern the difference between their thoughts and the Holy Spirit's voice. However, the discernment comes when the Holy Spirit finds us drawing near to him. That is when he will draw near to us and share with us the intimate things of Jesus' heart. He will also counsel us to become more like Jesus by telling us when we are both in and out of God's will. Then, to the degree that we obey his voice, we have greater intimacy with the Lord.

I'll never forget an incident during the early '70s when I was in prayer and heard the Holy Spirit ask me to make a chocolate pie for my neighbor. Hearing so precisely was new territory for me at the time, but I chose to obey. Sheepishly, I knocked on my neighbor's door and was surprised to discover that her eyes were red and swollen. I explained that God had told me to bake the pie and deliver it to her. She burst into tears and explained that just two hours before she had received word of her father's death. My obedience opened the door for me to pray with and minister to my neighbor.

One of my favorite works of the Holy Spirit is when he illumines the Word. The experience is so deep and so personal that you can't share it. You simply know that he is speaking to you. The Holy Spirit brings the Word of God to life and creates a hunger for more. Always record the Scripture, date it, and clearly describe what God told you so that you have a record to refer back to when you celebrate the victory.

Isaiah 11:2 provides seven names for the Holy Spirit, and these names describe the benefits he provides for us:

1. The Spirit of the Lord
2. The Spirit of Wisdom
3. The Spirit of Understanding
4. The Spirit of Counsel
5. The Spirit of Power
6. The Spirit of Knowledge
7. The Spirit of the Fear of the Lord

No matter what our need, the Holy Spirit is there to help us. That truth should bring us rest. Hudson Taylor described evidence of the Holy Spirit's control in a person's life as "no longer striving after faith, but resting in the Faithful One."

As we learn to lean on the Holy Spirit for our answers, we no longer work *for* our salvation, but he works *out* our salvation in and through us (Phil. 2:12). We then can echo Paul's confession, "It is no longer I who live, but Christ lives in me" (Gal. 2:20 NKJV). Openness and transparency before the scrutiny of the Holy Spirit develop the fruit of integrity and the joy of intimacy. It's his "into me see" that results in our intimacy.

## THE BIBLE

*British novelist David Lodge, in the introduction to one of his books, tells where he was [when he first heard of President Kennedy's assassination in 1963]—in a theater watching the performance of a satirical revue he had helped write. In one sketch, a character demonstrated his nonchalance in an interview by holding a transistor radio to his ear. The actor playing the part always tuned in to a real broadcast.*

*Suddenly came the announcement that President Ken-*
*nedy had been shot. The actor quickly switched it off, but it*
*was too late. Reality had interrupted stage comedy.*

*For many believers, the Scriptures are a nonchalant*
*charade. They don't expect anything significant to happen,*
*but suddenly God's reality breaks through, and they're*
*shocked.*[2]

Why? Because the Word of God is alive!

Martin Luther is quoted as saying, "The Bible is alive, it speaks to me; it has feet, it runs after me; it has hands, it lays hold of me." Yes, dear friend, reading it will cause God's reality to eventually break through, and that is when we experience our spiritual breakthroughs.

I'm convinced one reason believers avoid the Bible is that they approach it from a legalistic standpoint, a "have to," like being forced to do a boring homework assignment. However, those who approach the Bible from the standpoint of it becoming God's living love letter will open it and be changed by it.

Perhaps you've been challenged by a *One-Year Bible* but were unable to maintain the program. Daily, you get farther behind until you finally give up altogether, feeling guilty and unqualified to achieve the intimacy with God that you desire. Satan delights in watching believers despair in the things of the Lord. I'm sure he gets a great big belly laugh every time he sees a child of God give up on keeping up with the legalistic pace of those one-year plans. But the truth is that God is not about the quantity of our reading; he is about the change that our reading will create—a change toward intimacy.

It's in reading the Bible that we learn his character and know his heart. God does not love us more because we read his written

Word, but we learn to love him more when we do—and that's how intimacy deepens.

If you have been a Christian for any length of time, you probably know why Jesus called Satan the "father of lies," and said, "there is no truth in him" (John 8:44). Often, he comes to us with a thought that looks right and feels right and even sounds like God—but it's not. However, if we have the Word of God stored in our hearts, a verse will pop up and zing us with a truth. Then, that truth becomes a stone that we can fling at Satan to destroy him before we comply with his plan to destroy us.

In Psalm 119:11 David says, "I have hidden your word in my heart that I might not sin against you." I can't help but think of an appropriate quote by D. L. Moody: "The Bible will keep you from sin, and sin will keep you from the Bible."

Remember, as we discovered in an earlier chapter, Satan is not after our works, even our works of reading the Word; he's after our intimacy. And there is no greater gift that God has provided for developing intimacy than his written Word, the Bible. Of course when the Word comes alive in our hearts, another gift will unwrap more of our intimate experience with the Lord—the gift of worship.

## WORSHIP

We were born for worship. That's right. Everyone worships something or someone, because we all have a need to anchor our affections somewhere. I've noticed that people who don't worship God often set their affections on work, or sports, or substances, or things, or people, or even themselves. For the latter, theology is replaced with me-ology! The point is, worship is a focus of heart that results in an emotional response and a physical action.

For the Christian, worship says what we believe about God and how we have positioned him in our hearts. Authentic worship results in acts of obedience. Consider Abraham. He and wife Sarah had waited so long for a child that they were both beyond the age of childbearing. Sarah was ninety and hubby Abe had hit the ripe old age of one hundred. Imagine! After they waited so long for a child, you know little Isaac was the heartthrob of his parents. So along comes God with an invitation to take the boy on a trek up Mount Moriah to worship. Genesis 22:5 is the first time worship is talked about in the Bible. However, it's not mentioned, as we would expect, in reference to singing. Worship is mentioned in reference to obedience.

In this familiar passage, God asks Abraham to take his beloved boy Isaac up the mountain and to build an altar there so he can offer his son as a living sacrifice. Like the Son of God to come, Abraham's son would be asked to climb up on the altar and lay down his life. As you probably know, when Abraham lifted his arm to slay Isaac, the angel of the Lord stopped him. Then Abraham looked up, and standing in the thicket was the substitutional ram that God provided. Worship had been offered as obedience, and Abraham named the place "Jehovah Jireh," meaning "the Lord will provide." It's difficult to wrap our brains around such wholehearted trust. But intimates know that if we will be obedient, God will give us the strength we need to sacrifice whatever he requires of us in worship.

Another point to note in this story is that where there is worship, the Lord shows up with his presence. When we realize how much he loves us, we will welcome the worship on Mount Moriah.

For me, worship means setting aside time for God. Believe me, making time for the Lord is as much a sacrifice for me as it is for you. Sometimes I like to sit and tell God how much I adore him. Other times I sing, or listen to music, or just praise him for his goodness. Mostly, I just want to put the focus on him—that's the point of intimacy.

## PROPHECY

Actor Cary Grant once told how he was walking along a street and met a fellow whose eyes locked onto him with excitement. The man said, "Wait a minute, you're . . . you're—I know who you are; don't tell me—uh, Rock Hud . . . No, you're. . . ."

Grant thought he'd help him, so he finished the man's sentence: "Cary Grant."

And the fellow said, "No, that's not it! You're . . ."

There stood Cary Grant identifying himself with his own name in his own voice, but the fellow could not hear it.[3]

Sometimes we fail to recognize God's voice speaking in our midst because of preconceived ideas about who he is, or how his words should be packaged. Nonetheless, to be an intimate, and to have a personal relationship with him, we have to learn through experience. And one way he makes himself personal to us is through the prophetic word.

To illustrate, join me in looking at a few New Testament characters whose lives were transformed by a personal word from the Lord. In John 1, Jesus is in Galilee having just recruited Philip as a disciple. Philip dashes off to fetch Nathanael and to report that he has met the one whom the prophets wrote about from Nazareth. Nathanael retorts with the famous phrase, "Nazareth! Can anything good come from there?" (v. 46).

"Come and see for yourself" (v. 46 NLT), Philip nudges. We can read the rest of the account in John 1:47–49 in the *New Living Translation*:

*As they approached, Jesus said, "Now here is a genuine son*
*of Israel—a man of complete integrity."*
*"How do you know about me?" Nathanael asked.*
*Jesus replied, "I could see you under the fig tree before*
*Philip found you."*
*Then Nathanael exclaimed, "Rabbi, you are the Son of*
*God—the King of Israel!"*

One prophetic word and Nathanael entered into an experience with Jesus that would leave him forever changed. One
prophetic word nourished his hungry soul and captivated his
heart.

Sometimes God will speak a prophetic word of instruction.
For example, Simon Peter had fished all night with futile results.
That morning after ministering to the crowd, Jesus peered into
Peter's eyes and pierced his hopeless situation with prophetic
direction, "Put out into deep water, and let down the nets for a
catch" (Luke 5:4). Can't you just imagine what Peter's thinking?
*Is he kidding? I'm fished out! I dredged those barren waters all night*
*to no avail, and now he wants me to heave these heavy nets overboard*
*again? I'm hungry, exhausted, and my back is screaming for relief.*
But Peter heeded the word and reaped a catch so vast that the
nets bulged and tore from the overflow. One prophetic word of
instruction changed the course of Peter's life—forever!

Later, a confident Peter would vow never to defect. Then
came Jesus' prophetic warning: "I tell you, Peter, before the
rooster crows today, you will deny three times that you know
me" (Luke 22:34). And he did.

Prophetic words encourage, instruct, warn, guide, convict,
and console. When God gives you a prophetic word, it's as if
he is standing so close that you can feel the warm breath of his
voice blowing on your neck. Prophecy is God speaking directly

to you, and reading every part of your life. It's his intimate way of saying that he knows your address, no matter what you're going through.

When I'm out ministering, the Lord commonly gives me prophetic visions that touch the hearts of his people. Permit me to share an example. At a recent meeting, I encouraged those in search of prayer to come forward. Suddenly, I noticed a scruffy-looking man approaching. Above his head I saw a vision of nations flashing. I didn't know the man or what he did professionally so I merely spoke what I sensed the Lord saying. I began, "Sir, the Lord is saying he wants to restore the vision he gave you years ago. I hear him saying that you are a medical doctor [though he didn't look like one] and that you have plenty of money, but you are dissatisfied. What you are doing is not your heart cry." The man began to weep. "Sir, over your head I saw a picture of nation after nation appearing and disappearing—Cambodia, Vietnam, and Thailand, in particular. The Lord says you love to help people and that you desire to go to the nations. Does any of this make sense?"

He dropped to the floor and continued to sob. Finally, he answered, "Yes, I'm a doctor. I have been asking the Lord to send me to those three nations as a missionary, but I wasn't sure if that was his will." The prophetic vision brought confirmation and comfort to his heart. It also deepened his intimacy.

Another facet of the prophetic the Lord may use is dreams. Genesis 37:9 features the story of Joseph's dream in which he saw the sun, the moon, and eleven stars bowing down to him. Those elements of nature represented his father and brothers. As you probably know, the dream became a reality, and it may have helped him to persevere when he was sold to Egyptian slave traders, sent to Potiphar's house, and later falsely imprisoned.

Dreams come in all kinds of wrapping. I once had a prophetic "warning" dream in which a pastor Eddie and I knew well was having affairs and even trying to seduce me. In the dream he was devious and deceptive. I told Eddie about the dream the next morning, but neither of us understood it. However, three weeks later we learned that this pastor had seduced a recently widowed woman and that he was involved in other ungodliness. What began as a warning became a confirmation to me.

Last but not least, God often uses the Bible to speak a prophetic word. I've been through seasons when a certain passage leaped off the page and I simply couldn't get it out of my mind. Later, that passage proved to be a road map for navigating new territory in God.

Prophecy is God's idea. In 2 Chronicles 20:20 we read, "Believe His prophets, and you shall prosper" (NKJV). It saddens me to see much of the church trying to gag God's voice by silencing the prophetic. However, we must also use caution when giving and receiving prophetic words. There *will* be mistakes, but that fact should not mean we throw out the baby with the bath water. We don't do away with the role of pastor just because a few of them have neglected to handle the sheep properly. In fact, 1 Corinthians 13:9 explains that "we know in part and we prophesy in part." This verse has two meanings. First, nobody is completely perfect in prophesying, so the word must be judged. Second, God provides direction a little at a time so that we don't lose dependence on him.

Beware: The enemy may try to harpoon your heart and invalidate your intimacy with a false word. Remember, the devil is after your intimacy. I know of a woman named Carrie who received a prophetic word from a recognized prophet saying that if she did not act within two months, the purpose God had for her life would never happen. Carrie panicked, frozen in fear because she did not know what that purpose was. The false prophecy brought such death, confusion, and immobility that she could no longer hear God. She could no longer hear the gentle whisper of intimacy. She felt shamed and believed the Lord had forsaken her, so she lived in a barren wilderness of self-hatred for many years. Agreement with condemnation always results in self-hatred. If this has happened to you, forgive the one who gave the false word and refuse to close the door on God. Break the condemnation off of you and determine never to doubt God's love for you. He will never leave you or forsake you.

With regard to judging whether a word is from God or the flesh, the following criteria will prove to be helpful:

- Is the person who is prophesying credible?
- Do your spiritual mentors discern that the prophecy is correct?
- Does this prophecy bear witness with your heart?
- Is the Lord glorified by the prophecy?
- Does it contradict Scripture?
- Is it manipulative or controlling?
- Does it edify, exhort, and console rather than humiliate, condemn, or accuse? (See 1 Cor. 14:3.)

When you have judged the validity of the word, write it down. Then wait. If it's from the Lord and you are walking in his ways, prophecy will pave a path for you straight into the heart of God. Regardless of how long you have to wait, stand in faith until the promise is fulfilled.

## PRAYER

Time with God never returns void. An investment in prayer will draw you into intimacy if you stick with it. For me, prayer is the vehicle by which intimacy is maintained. But it wasn't always that way. When I first sought the Lord, I prayed and prayed, often feeling as though he was on vacation. For years, time in prayer was merely a case of being faithful for the sake of being faithful without any closeness to him. Finally, when I was just about to give up, he would sweep over me with floods of love so that I would continue to press in a while longer. I didn't understand then that he was establishing faithfulness in me.

My time was consumed with petitioning him for myself, or others, or even nations. I thought it was my responsibility to intercede for anyone and everyone who laid a burden on me. And even though I was receiving answers to prayer, I knew there had to be something more. After time, I no longer wanted him for the "goodies," I wanted to touch his goodness. I no longer cared about the benefits he could provide, I wanted the benefit of knowing him intimately.

The real shift occurred in 1984, when I sensed him asking, "Alice, what do you really want?" It was a penetrating question, and I knew that he would give me whatever I asked for.

"I just want more of you, Lord," I cried with utmost sincerity.

God's heart tore open and the joy of heaven exploded in me that day. I sensed his jubilation, "You asked for *me*! Alice, you could have asked for something *good*, but you asked for the *best*." On that memorable day, I transitioned from adolescent to mature love in Christ. I was forever a changed intimate of Christ! Of course, I still intercede, but jumping into his lap and cuddling up close to his heart has become effortless. It seems the burdens on my heart have been attended to on some new level, and most of my prayer time is just a matter of focusing my devotion on him.

Matthew 6:33 instructs us to "seek first his kingdom and his righteousness, and all these things will be given to you as well." When we seek God first, he provides all our physical needs.

So why don't people seek him and make prayer their daily priority? Probably because they don't feel qualified to share in his blessing. If I'm talking to you, be encouraged by the following. You're in good company.

- Moses stuttered.
- David's armor didn't fit.
- John Mark was rejected by Paul.
- Hosea's wife was a prostitute.
- Amos's only training was in the school of fig-tree pruning.
- Jacob was a liar.
- David had an affair.
- Solomon was too rich.
- Abraham was too old.
- David was too young.
- Timothy had ulcers.
- Peter was afraid of death.
- John was self-righteous.
- Naomi was a widow.
- Paul was a murderer. So was Moses.
- Jonah ran from God.
- Miriam was a gossip.
- Gideon and Thomas both doubted.
- Jeremiah was depressed and suicidal.
- Elijah was burned out.
- John the Baptist was a loudmouth.

- Martha was a worrywart. Mary was lazy.
- Samson had long hair.
- Noah got drunk.
- Did I mention that Moses had a short fuse? So did Peter, Paul . . . well, lots of folks did.

*But God doesn't require a job interview. He doesn't hire and fire like most bosses, because he's more our Dad than our Boss. He doesn't look at financial gain or loss. He's not prejudiced or partial, not judging, grudging, sassy, or brassy; he's not deaf to our cries, not blind to our needs.*

*As much as we try to earn them, God's gifts are free. We can do wonderful things and still not be WONDER-FUL. Satan says, "You're not worthy!" Jesus says, "So what? I AM!" Satan looks back and sees our mistakes. God looks back and sees the Cross. He doesn't calculate what you did in the past. It's not even on the record.*[4]

Sure, there are lots of reasons why the Lord wouldn't want to use us or share the depths of his heart with us. But he does. He wants you to develop your gifts and become an intimate.

# CHAPTER 7

# Intimacy and the Practice of Prayer

D. L. Moody is remembered for saying that every great move of God can be traced to a kneeling figure. I'm convinced that Moody was correct and that your move toward intimacy is dependent on practicing the discipline of prayer. Therefore, though we touched on the subject in chapter 6, I want to spend some extra pages sharing some keys I've used to unlock this power in my life.

## PRAYER HAS A HEAD CONNECTION

You know the old adage "running around like a chicken with its head cut off." Well, it's true! When a chicken's head is chopped off, it will race frantically about for a while, but eventually it will simply collapse. Frankly, nothing could more accurately describe the prayerless Christian. We were born to stay connected to the Lord through prayer, and without his headship, our frantic efforts to look effective will drop lifelessly to the ground.

Prayer is connecting your body to his head. You can't persevere in great things for God until you connect with your great God in prayer. Philippians 2:5 says, "Let this mind be in you which was also in Christ Jesus" (NKJV). Can you believe it? He will give us his mind if we diligently press in to his presence in prayer. Then it's no longer me, but Christ in me who is praying.

When you have the mind of Christ, you don't have to strive to hear his voice—it just flows. Conversely, when you have a blockage, you feel like Job, who said, "If only I knew where to find him; if only I could go to his dwelling!" (Job 23:3).

Nothing prevents us from finding him and dwelling in his presence more than a stronghold of unbelief. Permit me to explain. A stronghold is an impenetrable mindset, or house of thoughts, sometimes even a generational pattern of thinking that refuses change. At the root of this stronghold is a belief system of lies that sets self up as the authority rather than God. And when we are steeped in lies, we knowingly or unknowingly believe and behave in a way other than the way of faith that will accomplish God's results. The truth is that the spirit of unbelief will either cancel the power of faith, or faith will cancel the power of unbelief—but faith and unbelief cannot coexist. Therefore, when we have a stronghold of unbelief, we cannot have the mind of Christ.

Many of the people Moses led out of Egypt did not enter into the Promised Land because they had a spirit of unbelief. Hebrews 3:19 says, "Because of their unbelief they were not able to enter his rest" (NLT). And Hebrews 4:2 says, "The message they heard was of no value to them, because those who heard did not combine it with faith." When we pick and choose which parts of the Bible we will believe, we give the spirit of unbelief an opportunity to create a stronghold that destroys our ability to have intimacy.

Several years ago, I was teaching at a three-day conference. During the Friday-night ministry session, a beautiful young Scandinavian woman came forward for prayer. Talk about stoic. I felt as though I was praying for a stone. I knew I didn't have time to deal with the root of her need that first evening, so I prayed a short prayer for her and told her to come back on Saturday.

The following day I prayed, "Lord, please show me the root of this woman's problem." When I put my hands on her shoulders, I sensed the Lord saying that she had succumbed to a spirit of unbelief. I asked, "Have you or any of your family members struggled with atheism?" The woman confessed that both her father and grandfather had been atheists.

I asked her to renounce the spirit of unbelief and lies that produce doubt and confusion. Suddenly she began shaking violently and fell to the ground. Moments later, like a switch turned on, she was laughing and lighthearted. With a broad grin across her face, she exclaimed, "I feel God's love!"

Often those challenged with a stronghold of unbelief have had a traumatic experience with a father figure and have transferred that fear to God. Their hearts then have been hardened to the Lord so that intimacy can't be cultivated without prayer and soaking in God's truth.

People who are struggling with a spirit of unbelief are constantly dealing with negative self-talk and convincing themselves that they are unworthy to be loved or to receive from God. That lie takes up residence in the heart and becomes a stronghold that prevents intimacy. If you are dealing with the stronghold of unbelief, please open your eyes and make the following declaration with me:

"I renounce you, spirit of unbelief and spirit of lies, and I command you to leave my life right now. I break all covenants, vows, and agreements with you. I decree and declare that I am

79

no longer bound by your deception. I decree and declare that God's Son has set me free and that I am free indeed. In accordance with God's Word, I announce and proclaim that nothing is impossible with God; therefore, I am free to hear his voice and experience his love now."

If you have made this declaration, I encourage you to watch your words. Start confessing positive statements such as "God loves me" and "I am lovable" and "God desires to share his heart with me." The following are some Scriptures to memorize:

- "Everything is possible for him who believes" (Mark 9:23).
- "I am complete in Christ, who is head over all principalities and powers" (see Col. 2:10).
- "God can do anything, you know—far more than you could ever imagine or guess or request in your wildest dreams! He does it not by pushing us around but by working within us, his Spirit deeply and gently within us" (Eph. 3:20, THE MESSAGE).
- "Finally, brothers, whatever is true, whatever is noble, whatever is right, whatever is pure, whatever is lovely, whatever is admirable—if anything is excellent or praiseworthy—think about such things" (Phil. 4:8).

As you choose to replace the lies you have believed with the truth of God's Word, your feelings will catch up with your words and your intimacy will grow—big time! Believe me!

## PRAYER REQUIRES A GUIDE

None of us have the ability to get to God without the help of the Holy Spirit. I'm reminded of an occasion in the early '70s when Eddie and I had the privilege of meeting Mrs. James Stewart, the wife of the late author and evangelist Dr. James Stewart. Elderly, but still beautiful, Mrs. Stewart proudly affirmed a story told by the visiting preacher at the meeting we attended. The preacher retold it as if Mr. Stewart were speaking:

> *One afternoon I was visiting a famous European art gallery by myself. I was keenly disappointed and totally bored. I thought to myself,* Why do people come from all parts of the world to visit this place? *Sometime later I was invited by believers in that city to tour the same gallery as their guest. I wasn't very enthusiastic about it, considering my past experience. However, our host employed a guide, and under his skillful instruction, the paintings and tapestries in the gallery came alive. I was thrilled beyond words! I kept repeating, "Wonderful, wonderful, wonderful!" I asked one of the hostesses in the group what the difference was between this visit and my previous visit. She thought for a moment, and then with a beaming face said, "I see it now. It was the guide!"*

We can't develop an intimate prayer life apart from the Holy Spirit. He is our guide. Ask him to create a hunger in you for more of God—then get ready to be satisfied. Ask him to guide your time in prayer. The Lord has promised that he will: "But the Counselor, the Holy Spirit, whom the Father will send in my name, will teach you all things and will remind you of everything

I have said to you" (John 14:26). Ask the Holy Spirit to help you fall more in love with Jesus; he will not disappoint you.

## Practice Solitude

And speaking of getting away with him, Jesus taught us by example that intimacy is developed in the solitude of prayer. To be close to anyone, we must spend time alone with that person.

Solitude is a hardship when approached from a position of works, but when it is approached from a position of friendship, it's absolute joy. Jesus is "a friend who sticks closer than a brother" (Prov. 18:24), but we often hurry through life so fast that we forget to take our Friend with us. The distance between where we started out with him and where we end up then creates a void of loneliness. Our former solitude in prayer is now replaced with loneliness of heart. Jesus doesn't initiate the way back into closeness; we must choose it. The Bible says in James 4:8, "Draw near to God and He will draw near to you" (NKJV). Many of the church's greatest hymns are the outcome of solitude, such as "What a Friend We Have in Jesus." Here is the story:

> *Joseph Scriven watched in shock as the body of his fiancée was pulled from the lake. Their wedding had been planned for the next day. . . .*
>
> *Years later, in 1855, he received word that his mother was facing a crisis. Joseph wrote this poem and sent it to her. Mrs. Scriven evidently gave a copy to a friend who had it published anonymously, and it quickly became a popular hymn, though no one knew who had written it.*

*Meanwhile, Joseph fell in love again. But tragedy struck a second time when his bride, Eliza Catherine Roche, contracted tuberculosis and died in 1860, before their wedding could take place.*

*To escape his sorrow, Joseph poured himself into ministry, doing charity work for the Plymouth Brethren and preaching among the Baptists. He lived a simple, obscure life. . . . Ira Sankey later wrote:*

*"Until a short time before his death, it was not known that he had a poetic gift. A neighbor, sitting up with him in his illness, happened upon a manuscript copy of 'What a Friend We Have in Jesus.' Reading it with great delight and questioning Mr. Scriven about it, he said that he had composed it for his mother, to comfort her in a time of special sorrow, not intending that anyone else should see it. Some time later, when another Port Hope neighbor asked him if it was true that he had composed the hymn, his reply was, 'The Lord and I did it between us.' "[1]*

Solitude with God will eventually bring public honor, and things done in obscurity will often be brought out into the light.

## PRIME THE TIME

I'll never forget the summers growing up when we would visit my Uncle Bill and Aunt Claire Day, who lived on a farm in Nacogdoches, Texas, that had no indoor plumbing. They got their water to drink, wash clothes, and bathe from several outside water pumps. Sometimes in order to get the water flowing, we would need to prime the pump by adding water to it. Uncle Bill would pour water into the dry shaft. Then as he would thrust the handle up and down, the suction displaced the air, and water flowed freely from the deep reservoirs below the surface of the earth. Similarly, when God is not flowing through our prayers, there are things we can do to prime the spiritual pump.

The Bible says, "David *encouraged* himself in the Lord his God" (1 Sam. 30:6 KJV, emphasis added). Just two verses later we read, "So David inquired of the Lord, saying, 'Shall I pursue this troop? Shall I overtake them?' And He answered him, 'Pursue, for you shall surely overtake them and without fail recover all' " (NKJV). Priming his spirit during a difficult time gave David the courage to pray, and later in verses 18 and 19, we read that everything David had lost was restored.

Perhaps you are having trouble getting started in prayer. Let me encourage you. *Worship. Read a book, a devotional, a Scripture. Praise. Reflect on past victories.* Any of these can be used to restore the flow of prayer. Allow the Holy Spirit to show you how to encourage yourself in the Lord and prime the time for intimacy.

## REALIZE THAT PRAYER IS COMMUNION

My intimate experiences with the Lord have grown and changed throughout the years. So will yours. Jesus can't reveal everything to any of us at once; we grow closer to him over time. However, *prayer* is the word we use for having communion with Christ.

We tend to think of communion as relegated only to the Lord's Supper. The act sounds rather formal and somber; however, Jesus offers the broken bread and poured out wine so that we will *"re"-member* ourselves as part of his body. In other words, it's a way of examining our hearts and wherever we have felt disconnected, allowing him to show us how to make the connection again. We must meditate on Christ's sacrifice to "re"-member for the purpose of staying intimate.

And there is much more about the word *communion* that I want to cover here as a means of developing intimacy through prayer. For example, prayer is not just the quiet time spent in your prayer closet; it also includes making the Lord a part of your daily conversations. Assume his constant presence with you. Ask him to minister to people around you and through you. Ask him for revelation and counsel in every detail of your life from your interaction with the clerk at the store to what you watch on TV. Let all of your life become your prayer so that he communes with you and you commune with him about everything.

My friend, pastor and author Dutch Sheets, explains communion in this way:

*Second Corinthians 13:14 says, "The grace of the Lord Jesus Christ, and the love of God, and the fellowship of the Holy Spirit, be with you all." The word "fellowship" here is* koinonia *and is rich with meaning, as can be seen in the following definitions: The word* koinonia *implies that the Holy Spirit wants intimacy with us. This very word is used in 1 Corinthians 10:16 to describe the Lord's table, the bread and the wine. This is appropriate since it is the Lord's shed blood and broken body that brings us into covenantal, intimate communion with Him.*

*The Holy Spirit wants to commune with us. He has much to say if we learn to listen. He is the means to all revelation from God. He is the Teacher. He is a part of the*

*Godhead we're to be in relationship with. Let Him fellow-*
*ship and commune with you.*

*At times His fellowship with you requires no speaking.*
*Some communion is heart to heart. . . .*

*At times I crawl up to God for a look. Just knowing*
*He is looking back is enough. At other times He shares His*
*heart while I'm gazing.*

*There is an amazing picture of this sort of intimacy*
*in the following Scriptures: . . . "The secret of the* LORD *is*
*for those who fear Him, and He will make them know His*
*covenant" (Ps. 25:14, [emphasis] mine).*

*The words "secret" and "intimacy" are translated*
*from the same Hebrew word cowd, which means "couch,*
*cushion, or pillow."[2]*

The picture is of two intimate friends laughing and talking
at lunch in a crowded restaurant, oblivious to their surround-
ings, lost in their conversation. Or, it reminds me of my teen
slumber parties. Late at night, we girls would put on our PJs,
grab our pillows, and sit in a circle to talk, laugh, and tell stories.
The Lord desires this same kind of "snuggle close" friendship
with you, as if all of your life were an intimate prayer to share
together.

## INTIMATES LISTEN

And speaking of sharing, have you ever known a person
who simply wouldn't tolerate the idea of being quiet? I have. I
was acquainted with a woman who talked so incessantly that I
wondered how she ever developed intimacy with anyone. Perhaps
her constant babbling stemmed from her insecurity, or the fact

that she had to be in control at all times. I don't know. But I do know that good friends listen, especially those who want to live prayerfully close to the Lord.

I often laugh to myself as I watch my friend's dog, Chester, mindlessly run off while she chases and continues to call his name. He behaves as if he is completely deaf. But when she shouts, "Let's go bye-bye!" he turns on a dime and dashes for the car. Sadly, the body of Christ is often just as selective with its hearing as that little dog. We get so used to tuning God out that when he has something special to speak into our lives, we're too distracted to hear him.

At least five times in the New Testament we read, "He who has ears to hear, let him hear." It doesn't say let him talk, but hear. If only we would learn to listen. Listening is always key to developing intimacy in prayer!

## PRAYER DIFFERS FROM INTERCESSION

I am often asked, "What is the difference between prayer and intercession?" Let me start by saying that you can pray without intimacy, but you cannot intercede without it. Intercession is praying the burdens of God's heart. Prayer, however, is talking to the Lord; it is the way in which intimacy is developed. Prayer is also the way we live our daily lives in him—keeping our ears tuned toward him, sharing our thoughts with him, and practicing his presence.

Back in the 1600s there lived a man named Nicholas Herman who was greatly influenced by his parish priest named Lawrence. Young Nicholas served as a soldier and was injured in battle. Later, he entered the monastic life and took the name Lawrence in honor of his mentor. He worked in the kitchen washing dishes and practicing the presence of God. He shunned the limelight and sought satisfaction only in the fulfilling of

God's will, whether "by suffering or consolation"[3]—it did not matter.

Brother Lawrence changed his world by demonstrating for others how to be wholly devoted and how to govern life by love without selfish views. In the book *The Practice of the Presence of God*, Brother Lawrence says,

> *There is not in the world a kind of life more sweet and delightful than that of a continual conversation with God. Only those can comprehend it who practice and experience it. Yet I do not advise you to do it from that motive. It is not pleasure which we ought to seek in this exercise. Let us do it from a principle of love, and because it is God's will for us. Were I a preacher, I would, above all other things, preach the practice of the presence of God. Were I a director, I would advise all the world to do it, so necessary do I think it, and so easy too. Ah! knew we but the want we have of the grace and assistance of God, we would never lose sight of Him, no, not for a moment. . . . I do not advise you to use many words and long discourses in prayer, because they are often the occasions of wandering. Hold yourself in prayer before God, like a dumb or paralytic beggar at a rich man's gate. Let it be your business to keep your mind in the presence of the Lord.[4]*

I'm reminded of a dear saint of God that I knew who lived in such harmony with the Father that when we talked she had difficulty at times sorting out the conversations. She would say, "Alice, when you come to. . . . Yes, Lord. I will tell her that in a moment. . . . Alice, as I was saying, when you come to. . . ." She was carrying on simultaneous conversations with the Lord and me. And because of the level of holiness on which she lived, it didn't even seem odd to her. That, my friend, is the intimacy of prayer!

CHAPTER 8

# Rewards for Intimacy

She was the cutest "wienie dog" ever. Schotze (German for "little treasure") was our family's delight. As a puppy she would get excited when the kids wandered through the house. With ears pinned back and a high-pitched squeal, short-legged Schotze would run wildly from room to room seeking the kids for some fun. In a word, she was—*adorable.*

And smart? I've never seen a smarter dog than our Schotze. We taught her to roll over, sit up, go outside, and even speak. Really! Our second son was convinced that he'd taught her to say his name, "Bryan," in a puppy voice. And guess what? It really did sound as though she was saying Bryan's name! Okay, it sorta sounded like his name.

Eddie cut a hole in the brick wall of our home and created a doggie door for Schotze so she could go out to chase squirrels in the yard or stay inside in the den to sit near the fireplace. She had instant access to any place in our home. When I arrived home and entered through the back door, our little Schotze would dance and twirl around and around in sheer delight. She loved us and longed to be in our presence. She loved one special treat most of all, so we would give Schotze her heart's desire—cheese! Oh, she squealed with delight when the cheese came out of the refrigerator.

Similarly, God also provides rewards for those who love him and diligently seek his presence. In this chapter, we'll explore *just a few* of the rewards for intimacy because I don't want to spoil any of your future surprises.


## FAVOR

As a teenager I attended school with lots of conscientious kids, but only a few ever walked in favor. We referred to them as "teacher's pets." The teacher appeared to like those students more than the others and would give them extra privileges and attention. In the same way, even though God loves all of us, the Lord's intimates have so earned his trust that they receive extra privileges and attention too.

When you are experiencing God's favor, you are singled out for a blessing because you have been close and dependable in his sight. People with God's favor carry his influence and become magnets for attracting others to help them accomplish God's purposes and plans. Jesus had favor with God and man, and we can have that same kind of attraction too. When you have favor, people listen to you, and they want to cooperate with what the Lord is doing in your life.

God's favor not only draws people to you for larger purposes, but it also creates opportunities in the daily details of life. For example, in 1999 Eddie and I had been teaching at Spiritual Outreach, a ministry led by our close friend Mosy Madugba in Nigeria. Our travel schedule had been very busy for several months. We had been teaching for six days for a group of nearly fourteen thousand pastors. Eddie and I were glad to go home because we were exhausted and longing to sleep in our own bed.

We had paid our own way to Nigeria and traveled coach. You can imagine our surprise when we arrived at the airport and discovered that the airline had given away our seats. Disappointed doesn't begin to describe our feelings at that moment. We prayed, "Lord, please grant us your favor." Other passengers experiencing the same predicament were angry and out of control. Our patience was sorely tested too, but we determined to be Christlike. Eddie asked the woman behind the counter for help. A Nigerian flight attendant overheard him and pulled us aside, offering to transfer us to another airline. She even arranged first-class seats without an extra charge. Why did we make it when others didn't? I believe our experience is an example of God's favor.

When you have favor, people who would otherwise not give you a second thought or seek you out suddenly take notice. Favor creates a place for you. It makes a way where there is no way. It gives you a voice—not just for your personal use but also to advance the purposes of God in the lives of others. Consider Esther's story. When Queen Vashti was deposed for refusing to obey her husband King Ahasuerus, a search ensued for the most beautiful young virgins in the land. Enter Esther, a lovely young woman who had been raised by her uncle Mordecai. Picture this: She was a Jewish beauty chosen from thousands to become a Persian (today that would be Iranian) queen. If that isn't remarkable enough, her religious and national identity remained hidden until God could use her to save her race from extinction. Esther 2:15 reports that "Esther won the favor of everyone who saw her."

Esther was a woman of prayer and fasting, a woman who willingly agreed to lay down her life for God's purposes. Her level of commitment to the Lord and his people not only paved the way for her to be in the right place at the right time, but it also brought a level of favor that even her enemies could not extinguish. Like Esther, if you are an intimate, God will single you out for an appointed purpose at an appointed time, and you will see the reward of favor opening the doors for you.

## WISDOM

Another reward for intimacy is wisdom. It's been said that you can be knowledgeable with another man's knowledge, but you cannot be wise with another man's wisdom. The reason: God *is* wisdom. Proverbs 30:3 says, "I have not learned wisdom, nor have I knowledge of the Holy One." Unless we know God, we cannot know wisdom.

Intimates have learned that according to Psalm 111:10, "The fear of the Lord is the beginning of wisdom." And Proverbs 9:10 goes on to say, "The fear of the Lord is the beginning of wisdom, and knowledge of the Holy One is understanding." So let's define the fear of the Lord according to Scripture. Proverbs 8:13 says, "To fear the Lord is to hate evil." In other words, wisdom is the result of agreeing with God and hating what is evil. As we grow in intimacy, it becomes increasingly more difficult to sin because we don't want to love anything that separates us from God's presence—and sin separates.

It's easy to identify wisdom in an intimate's life. It shows up in an ability to understand the things of God. It is also evidenced in right responses and accurate answers. Remember Solomon? In 1 Kings 3, God gave him a dream in which the Lord said, "Ask! What shall I give you?" (v. 5 NKJV). Solomon set his own desires aside and replied, "Give to Your servant an understanding heart to judge Your people, that I may discern between good and evil" (v. 9 NKJV). Wisdom understands how to deal with both good and evil, and it can discern the presence of both.

I'll share a personal illustration here to emphasize my point. It was a time in which God gave me supernatural wisdom for detecting something evil. In 1990 I was in Israel on a ministry tour where I met Lilliana, an Argentinean Jew who gave her heart to the Lord. God told me to go to a Christian organization where Lilliana worked. When I told her that God had sent me on a prophetic prayer journey to do spiritual mapping and that I was going to pray on the Mount of Olives, Lilliana was concerned. After explaining that the land was under Arab control, she generously offered to take me there. The following day Lilliana wanted to go to the post office before leaving on our trip. It was about midday, and we stood for quite a while awaiting our turn. We had not reached the front of the line when I sensed the Lord saying, "Get out NOW. Right now!" I turned to Lilliana and insisted on leaving immediately. She could see the intensity on my countenance, so we barreled out of there. A short time later an explosion occurred in the post office.

I have learned through many experiences to recognize and heed these urgent promptings from the Holy Spirit. Remember, delayed obedience in any form is disobedience, and it can result in devastating consequences.

Another word of caution: Most of us can be tempted to turn to other people for our wisdom. However, taking a poll usually creates confusion. We can choose to collect as many opinions as needed to reason our way out of problems, but godly wisdom will only come from a place of intimacy in the Lord. Proverbs 3:5 instructs us not to lean on our own understanding but rather to acknowledge the Lord and let him guide us. When I say that, people often respond with, "What about finding wisdom in many counselors like it says in Proverbs 15:22?" Counselors can only confirm God's will; they can't create it. When you do what God wants you to do, you will have success—and that's another reward for intimacy.

## ANOINTING

Of course, one of the most amazing rewards for being an intimate is the anointing, which is the presence of God flowing through you with his power, strength, wisdom, counsel, or anything else you need. The anointing has been described as God putting his *super* on your *natural*, and then letting him move supernaturally through you. In my case, I think of it as transforming from plain ol' ordinary Alice to Alice Smith, Wonder Woman!

Many Christians have been under the anointing and not even known it. For example, have you ever been advising someone when all of a sudden you are saying such profound things that you wish you could record them? That's the anointing—God supernaturally speaking through you.

Several years ago I went to a Denny's restaurant to grab a quick late lunch. I could see that the middle-aged waitress who was about to take my order looked quite sad. "What is your name?" I asked. Suddenly I felt the anointing welling up in me. Without hesitation, I began telling her that she was much loved by God. Tears spilled down her cheeks as I spoke. "The Lord said that he is aware of the major betrayal you have just experienced, and it was not your fault. You have wondered if life is worth living anymore. You have even questioned God's love for you and asked if he cares. He does. The Lord says he will take care of you and your children."

Because there were only two other customers in the restaurant, I asked her if we could pray together. She welcomed the prayer, and we both cried under the anointing of God's presence. This dear lady then confided that her husband of twenty years had committed adultery and abandoned her for the other woman. Having never worked outside the home, she was now struggling to support herself and two children. I knew the Lord was leading my words so I just followed his impressions in my mind. The waitress recommitted her life to Christ, and I heard the Lord nudge me to give her a three-hundred-dollar tip. I called Eddie and he agreed we should do so.

In this instance, anointing came in the form of a word of knowledge. Of course, that's not the only way the anointing shows up. In my prayer closet, his immanent and abiding presence comes. When it does, it's as though time has stopped, or perhaps that I have stepped outside of time. I lose the desire for anything other than being in his presence, and I feel a tugging in my spirit to go deeper with him until he simply envelops me.

I've come to realize that as our dependence upon God deepens, our level of anointing will also increase. However, if we have the attitude that we are going to control the Lord, we prevent the anointing. Remember in Luke 10:38–42, when the Lord was invited to Martha's house, and Mary sat at his feet instead of helping with the dinner preparations? Martha was distracted with the details of *how* to visit rather than focusing on *who* was there to visit. Before long she was ordering the Lord around, "Lord, . . . tell her to help me!" So Jesus put the whole situation in perspective: " 'Martha, Martha,' the Lord answered, 'you are worried and upset about many things, but only one thing is needed. Mary has chosen what is better, and it will not be taken away from her.' "

Jesus is impressed with relationship. He is about intimacy. If we draw close, so will he. In John 12:32, Jesus gives us a clue for drawing close: "But I, when I am lifted up from the earth, will draw all men to myself." If you are not experiencing the anointing, ask yourself, "Who or what is being lifted up here on earth?"

During ministry times at the altar, I'm there to give myself away for the Lord in any way he chooses. When the anointing falls, I can minister for hours. Then, when his power lifts, I'm so fatigued in my own strength that I'd welcome a stretcher to carry me out.

Your experiences will probably be different from mine because God shows up and does what he does, and we can only be available to receive and follow his leading. The anointing is never the result of a formula. It's the manifestation of God's desire to bless his people with his presence. And lest any of us consider ourselves better than others because the Lord has chosen to use us, remember that God uses anyone or anything that is available. In Numbers 22, Balaam is so focused on his own agenda that God even anoints the donkey to deliver a message and save Balaam from making a bad choice.

In Matthew 27, Jesus was brought before Governor Pilate for sentencing. "While Pilate was sitting on the judge's seat, his wife sent him this message: 'Don't have anything to do with that innocent man, for I have suffered a great deal today in a dream because of him' " (v. 19). Tragically, Pilate didn't listen to her warning, but the point remains—God will use any willing person.

God works through people to protect others, and he can use the wheat, the tares, and the "who cares" to do so. If he can speak through a donkey, he can anoint any of us to deliver his message or fulfill his plans. It's not about the vessel; it's about the Lord having a vessel to work through to accomplish his purposes.

Zig Ziglar said, "Right attitude, right altitude." When our attitude is right, God can raise us up and anoint us to do just about anything. But when we are all about self-promotion, we'll be brought down. We don't minister to get the glory; we get the glory to minister for him.

In Matthew 4, we read that Jesus fasted forty days and was tempted three times by Satan. Any of us would probably have given in, but Jesus did not. Why? He put nothing before his desire to glorify the heavenly Father. Jesus left the wilderness with greater anointing because he understood the necessity of intimacy.

## SECRETS

President Ronald Reagan, while addressing a class of high school graduates, joked that the first thing he did when he became president was to have his high school transcripts classified "Top Secret." Another noted statesman, Benjamin Franklin, said, "Three people can keep a secret if two of them are dead." Everyone has secrets, but not everyone has a way to keep them confidential. Tell me whom you trust with your secrets, and I'll tell you who your intimates are.

God has confidants too. Psalm 25:14 explains that "the secret of the Lord is with those who fear Him, and He will show them His covenant" (NKJV).

A secret is a covenant, a trust of something highly prized in someone's heart. Secrets carry both privilege and responsibility. They can represent the rewards of intimacy, but also the potential of betrayal. Shared secrets are broken trusts. Therefore, most of us wouldn't dream of revealing our personal secrets to anyone who hasn't proven his or her character. It's the same way in friendship with the Lord. Faithfulness must be cultivated and tested before he will entrust to us the things closest to his heart.

Please don't misunderstand: There is a huge disparity between impurity and immaturity. God has plenty of grace for the *immature* Christian who is growing in intimacy. But for those who are *impure*, those with a prideful spirit, he does not share a confidence. Mark 4:11 assures us that "the secret of the kingdom of God has been given to you. But to those on the outside everything is said in parables."

99

What better illustration than that of Samuel? You may recall that Samuel was the long-awaited child of Hannah and Elkanah. He had been dedicated to the service of the Lord prior to his birth. Therefore, when Samuel was old enough to leave his mother, he was presented to the Lord and sent to live with Eli, the priest, at the tabernacle.

However, Eli's sons, Hophni and Phinehas, had no respect for God. They seduced the young women who assisted at the entrance to the tabernacle, stole money from the people, dishonored their father, and disgraced the sacrifices of the Lord. These two young men were scoundrels, so God purposed in his heart to destroy them and make sure that no one in their line ever served in ministry again. Serious stuff, huh?

Meanwhile, the young boy Samuel assisted Eli in the things of the Lord. Now in those days few people ever received messages or visions. But one night, while Samuel was sleeping in the tabernacle near the ark of God, the Lord began to call his name. At first, Samuel was confused, thinking Eli was summoning him. He awakened the priest and asked what he needed. This scenario was repeated several times, because Samuel had never before received a word from the Lord. Eventually Eli realized that it was God speaking to Samuel, so he instructed him to go back to bed and answer the Lord directly. When he did, the Lord began to pour his heart out to Samuel, saying, "I am about to do a shocking thing in Israel. I am going to carry out all my threats against Eli and his family, from beginning to end. I have warned him that judgment is coming upon his family forever, because his sons are blaspheming God and he hasn't disciplined them. So I have vowed that the sins of Eli and his sons will never be forgiven by sacrifices or offerings" (1 Sam. 3:11–14 NLT).

Can you imagine receiving a message like that about your mentor and then living to see it come to pass? That would put the fear of the Lord in anyone! It certainly did with Samuel. He stayed close to the heart of God from then on. As he grew, Samuel learned to hold God's secrets and not to share information unless the Lord commanded him to do so. The process of maturity took many years; however, intimacy with God proved to be worth the investment. Samuel eventually became the last of the judges and the first of the prophets. He succeeded Eli in the priestly office and became the first major prophet. He also anointed both Saul and David as kings and became spiritual advisor to both. Samuel loved, listened to, and leaned on the Lord. He was one of God's secret service agents.

My life in God's service began early too. At fifteen years old, I was saved and heard the Lord's voice, "You will be a minister and an intercessor for me." I assumed he meant leading a children's choir or teaching Sunday school, not being a licensed and ordained minister. In my twenties, I supposed he also meant being a sidekick to whatever Eddie was doing. I was known for my singing voice and ministered musically with him most of the time. Like most women in my generation, I held the conviction that the female gender could only play second fiddle and that they were forbidden to do anything else.

Undoubtedly, the reason I didn't see the fulfillment of God's word until 1995 is that I couldn't have handled it before then. I would first need to shake off and break off the traditions I had ascribed to women in ministry. All of my old paradigms had to shift.

As I've said earlier in this book, God knows how to bring his word to pass without our self-promoting assistance. We are simply required to hold his secrets until he releases us to share them. The more we are faithful to listen and obey, the more he will reveal to us.

If he's given you a word about your future, let him bring it to pass. Learning to wait on the Lord is the way we develop humility. Jacob's son Joseph received a vision, but he immaturely revealed it before its time. The result: His brothers became jealous and tried to destroy him. Years of waiting and breaking ensued before Joseph became the humble prime minister of Egypt that God had intended him to be.

Secrets should not make us weird, nor do they come without a level of responsibility. They carry a sense of favor, but they can also be twisted into the practice of pride. I learned that lesson the hard way.

In 1989 at the hotel with Charlene, when I had that incredible visitation from God (see chapter 2), I received a powerful prophetic word about Eddie. I went home and notified him that the Lord had told me something about his future but that I was not free to share it with him. He responded as if I thought I was more spiritual, which probably hurt him deeply. How condescending, condemning, and completely immature I was then! It didn't take more than one mistake to learn that God does not share his secrets with us so we can flaunt the friendship. We're not doing God any favors by trying to act mystical when we get words that others don't. Remember, Satan had a high position in heaven, but pride brought him low. Never again do I want to be in a position where God must knock me down to teach me a lesson. Since that early incident, I've learned to stay on my face in my prayer closet as much as possible. My motto: You can't fall off the floor!

God is not about titles, or celebrity, or making elitists out of any of us. He's looking for close friends who know how to keep a secret.

## Answers to Prayer

One of the great rewards of staying close to the Lord is watching him provide answers to prayer. I mean, if your best friend needed help, wouldn't you do everything in your power to make a difference? Of course you would. And when we're feeling helpless, there's nothing quite like having a close connection with someone in a powerful position. Yep! It's not what you know, but the One you know that matters.

Having read numerous biographies from the past century, I've noticed that God's intimates received results with a consistency that is seemingly uncommon in today's Christian community. For example, there's George Müller, an ordinary man with an extraordinary connection to God. For more than half a century during England's most impoverished times, Müller ran the Ashley Downs orphanages that he founded in Bristol, England. He provided for more than ten thousand orphans at a cost that exceeded eight million dollars without ever mentioning his need to anyone other than God.

Numerous times the children would sit down to dinner with nothing on their plates but faith. Then Müller would pray. Without fail, there came a knock on the door to meet that day's need. I love the story in which the milk truck broke down right in front of the orphanage. The milkman's loss became the Lord's provision. God always takes care of his intimates. I wonder why we have such difficulty experiencing his answers to prayer today.

Perhaps the answer has something to do with the "Hokey Pokey." Remember the old song and dance? "You put your right foot in, you put your right foot out . . . you do the hokey pokey and you turn yourself about." Today's church is quite adept at doing this sort of dance with God. We bring just enough of ourselves under his lordship to feel good about being in the Kingdom, but we don't want to give up all of self. One day we want to be intimate with the Lord, the next day we find ourselves torn between serving him and serving our selfish desires. And we can't understand why God doesn't answer our prayers!

People such as George Müller had only one focus. God was his all in all. Like the apostle Paul, who experienced answered prayer, we too must say, "I consider everything a loss compared to the surpassing greatness of knowing Christ Jesus my Lord" (Phil. 3:8). If developing intimacy with God is the most important thing in our lives, consistent answers to prayer will become automatic. It's okay to be a name-dropper when the only name you rely on is God's.

# JOY

Back in the '80s we sang a rendition of "Down in My Heart." One chorus began with, "I have the joy of Jesus, joy of Jesus, down in my heart." My friend would giddily respond, "Well, why not tell your face!" And now that I think about it, she was right. Too many Christians have lost their ability to smile and share the joy of Jesus with others. But you can always identify the intimates; they're the ones with the joy down in their hearts and all over their faces.

In the *King James Version*, John 7:38 describes a person who really believes God as one "out of [whose] belly shall flow rivers of living water." And I'm sure we've all met people like that. There's an effervescence about these people that is contagious. The life of the Lord just seems to well up with emotion in them—kind of like the pressure that is produced by those great big soda machines. It just keeps bubbling up and flowing out.

There is, however, a difference between happiness and joy. Happiness is dependent on what is happening, while joy depends on the One in whom we place our trust. God said, "Never will I leave you; never will I forsake you" (Heb. 13:5). That kind of assurance should spawn deep excitement and a longing to love him more. Joy doesn't emanate from outward conditions;

it comes from the contentment of knowing that Jesus has you covered—no matter what you're facing.

Consider Paul and Silas. They were severely beaten, thrown into a dungeon, and bound in shackles with chains. Most of us would've been demanding to speak to our congressman or grumbling about such mistreatment—but not Paul and Silas. They were intimates with Jesus. So they did what intimates do: they let the joy of Jesus well up into prayer and started singing hymns of praise to God. They knew that God knew exactly where they were. He did. He even sent an earthquake to shake the building and loosen their chains (Acts 16:22–26).

Unlike Paul and Silas, some of us are in self-imposed prisons, places of such discontent that even God can't break through the walls of our own making. I'm reminded of Viktor Frankl, a doctor who survived the Nazi concentration camps. Dr. Frankl said that those who gave their bread away despite their own hunger and those who chose to encourage others were the only ones to survive. He said they had learned a truth: The one thing no one can take away from us is our right to choose our attitude. Let's choose to be contented in every circumstance and focus on our intimacy with God.

Everything you are going through right now will eventually come to an end, but your relationship with the Lord will last forever. My friend Pamela told me about a bumper sticker she saw recently. It read: "Don't take life so seriously—it's not permanent!" It's true. But the relationship you cultivate with the Lord is everlasting. The final rewards for intimacy will produce a smile on your face and a joy you can carry in your heart forever.

# CHAPTER 9

# Intimacy In Action

Perhaps you've read my favorite short story, "The Gift of the Magi," by O. Henry. It takes place the day before Christmas. All of Della's efforts to save enough money for Jim's present have added up to a mere dollar and eighty-seven cents. Jim and Della own only two things in which they take pride: for Della, a long flowing head of hair that cascades from her crown to well below her knees. For Jim, a gold watch that had been his father's and before that his grandfather's.

True lovers can be financially destitute and still find ways to give. And so with little time to spare, Della frantically races off to the hair goods shop, where she sells her shiny brown locks for twenty dollars. She then ransacks the stores to hit upon the perfect gold chain for Jim's prized pocket watch. Della finds one worthy. Twenty-one dollars. Briskly and contentedly, she dashes toward home with only eighty-seven cents tucked in her pocket.

Meanwhile, Jim has remembered the beautiful tortoiseshell combs that Della so longed for in the window of a Broadway shop. He sells his cherished watch to buy them, then heads home for Christmas Eve dinner. Jim is taken aback as he opens the door to their shabby little apartment. There stands Della with a closely cropped, boyish haircut. He hands her the gift, and she clutches it with gratitude. Della asks to see his gold watch so that she can add the glistening new chain to it. Tears flow. Hearts openly intertwine.

O. Henry concludes:

> *The magi, as you know, were wise men—wonderfully wise men—who brought gifts to the Babe in the manger. They invented the art of giving Christmas presents. Being wise, their gifts were no doubt wise ones, possibly bearing the privilege of exchange in case of duplication. And here I have lamely related to you the uneventful chronicle of two foolish children in a flat who most unwisely sacrificed for each other the greatest treasures of their house. But in a last word to the wise of these days, let it be said that of all who give gifts these two were the wisest. Of all who give and receive gifts, such as they are wisest. Everywhere they are wisest. They are the magi.[1]*

Intimacy is the result of a choice to let someone see into your heart and live there with you. You can love your neighbor enough to rescue him from a burning building, but that doesn't mean the two of you will ever have an intimate relationship. To experience genuine intimacy, both people must choose to trust, be vulnerable, and invest in each other all they have.

## MOTIVES OF THE HEART

Actions can be misleading. I once thought they could be trusted without scrutiny. That was naïve. After several betrayals,

I have learned the hard way (the way everyone learns) that motives must be examined.

The Bible says, "Man looks at the outward appearance, but the Lord looks at the heart" (1 Sam. 16:7). Yes, we look at what is done, but God looks at why we did it. Most of us judge what we believe to be the intentions of another person's heart—which we cannot see—but seldom do we look at the reasons for our own actions.

When was the last time you asked yourself why you are following the Lord? It seems a peculiar question, but the answer is necessary for developing real intimacy.

You see, when we desire intimacy for the sake of earning God's love and/or rewards or escaping his punishment, we step out of relationship with him and into the bondage of legalism. Then we can potentially become condemning, judgmental, and prideful because all our actions are based on the fear, loss, and punishment that broken rules bring.

We fear not *being* enough, as if the Christian life were dependent on who we are rather than on whom the Savior became for us. We fear not *doing* enough, as if our inheritance were dependent on what we've earned rather than what we have gained through Christ's sacrifice. We even fear what others won't achieve based on our own prideful control. Consequently, we drive them away from God rather than loving them enough to let them make their own decisions.

That's what happened to Eddie and me. We were often too structured, too "rules" oriented. We erroneously believed that by insisting on church attendance and holding the reins tightly, we could produce godly character in our children. Perhaps you've been there and learned as we did that sometimes too many rules can create resentment. We have since learned to express unconditional love for our children and grandchildren, even when they disappoint us with unwise decisions. Doing this has drawn them into a closer walk with Jesus. Love for God is the result of knowing he loves you, no matter what you've done or how many times you've fallen short. This is a wonderful truth for all of us to remember!

The reason we come to faith is that we feel so freed from the penalty we deserve for breaking God's laws and from our feelings of worthlessness. We hear that faith is a gift, that we are accepted, and that we were loved even when we were still in sin—and we can't wait to tell the world. Just a few years later, however, rather than resting in the security of God's love, we may find ourselves relentlessly striving to obey, working for recognition, and feeling that we don't measure up.

Subtly but surely, we step out of the grace walk of God's unconditional love and enter instead into a religious mode of earning rewards and hoping to avoid punishment. At this point, we see God no longer as a loving father but rather a harsh judge—and we become just like the person we imagine him to be. We even second-guess his intentions toward us.

## THE LAW KILLS INTIMACY

When Jesus walked the earth, he was accused of loving sinners. Everywhere he went, he forgave people's sins and set them free from shame and guilt. But the religious leaders hated Jesus because he broke the rules in order to help people and refused to condemn anyone for anything other than being unloving.

Jesus clashed with and was finally killed by a group of religious zealots called the Pharisees. The word *Pharisee* actually means "separated ones." They were separated from people in order to study the laws, the traditions, and the rituals of their Jewish heritage. They controlled the synagogues and the people, and transformed Judaism from a religion of sacrifice to one of law—both of which relied on man's works rather than God's mercy. The Pharisees used the law to extract money from individuals and taught that perfectionism, or perfect obedience to the letter of the law, would earn answers to prayer.

Now you might be reading this and thinking, *Who cares? Get to the point!* Am I right? Well, here's the truth: If you are lacking intimacy, there's a Pharisee in you that needs to be evicted.

The Pharisee hides in all of us in places of the heart where we hear ourselves saying:

- I would never . . .
- How could he . . . ?
- You should have . . .
- If only I would have, or could have . . .

I remember talking to a brilliant young pastor who said that women in pantsuits were never allowed to speak in his church. I asked, "If a pastor from Scotland visited wearing a kilt, would you let him speak in a skirt?" These are man's laws, and they are ridiculous! It's not the outward things that condemn us; it's the judgmental attitudes of the heart. The law of heaven is love, and anything that is contrary to love has a root of legalism, a Pharisee, in it. Legalism is cruel and intolerant, but Jesus' love is always there to forgive and restore people. The laws of sin and death kill, but the law of the Spirit of life sets us free (Rom. 8:2).

In Romans 8:1 we read, "There is now no condemnation for those who are in Christ Jesus." In other words, if we are in Christ, we don't take condemnation in, nor do we give it out. It's not how many pages of the Bible we read, or whether our neighbor is part of a different denomination, that matters most. The Christian life is not about judging others, or even ourselves, for the purpose of being condemning—it's about letting God's love in so we can let it out again. Our role is not to do the work of the Holy Spirit. Conviction must come from God.

One reason we go through suffering is so we can learn how to love. When we judge God as unfair, or a person as undeserving, we will need to be touched by pain to conquer the Pharisee in our hearts.

Remember Job? He offered sacrifices for his kids in religious ways, hoping to make up for their lack of commitment to God (Job 1:4-5). He was focused on obedience to the law. And though he was better than most at keeping the law, it was Job's heart that God was after. We don't sacrifice to be loved. We are loved; therefore, we sacrifice. Neither do we serve to earn love. We are loved; therefore, we serve.

The Greek word for grace is *charis*, meaning the unmerited favor of God. In other words, you and I are blessed with special treatment just because we belong to him. And that sense of belonging makes life no longer about striving not to sin, but rather being free from the desire to sin because we know that we are loved.

The following chart explains the difference between the law and grace.[2]

| The law says, *Do* this and you shall live. | The gospel says, *Live* and then you shall do. |
|---|---|
| The law says, *Pay* me what you owe. | The gospel says, I frankly *forgive* you all. |
| The law says, *Make* yourself a new heart and a new spirit. | The gospel says, A new heart will I *give* you and a new spirit will I put within you. |

| | |
|---|---|
| The law says, You shall love the Lord your God with all your heart, and with all your soul, and with all your mind. | The gospel says, Herein is love, not that we loved God, but that He loved us and sent His son to be the propitiation for our sins. |
| The law says, *Cursed* is every one who continues not in all things written in the book of the law to do them. | The gospel says, *Blessed* is the man whose iniquities are forgiven, and whose sins are covered. |
| The law says, The *wages* of sin is death. | The gospel says, The *gift* of God is eternal life through Jesus Christ our Lord. |
| The law *demands* holiness. | The gospel *gives* holiness. |
| The law says, *Do*. | The gospel says, *Done*. |
| The law *extorts* the unwilling service of a bondman. | The gospel *wins* the loving service of a son and freeman. |
| The law makes blessings the result of *obedience*. | The gospel makes obedience the result of *blessings*. |
| The law places the day of rest at the end of the week's work. | The gospel places it at its beginning. |
| The law says, *If*. | The gospel says, *Therefore*. |
| The law was given for the *restraint* of the old man. | The gospel was given to bring *liberty* to the new man. |
| Under the law, salvation was *wages*. | Under the gospel, salvation is a *gift*. |

If we believe that we are loved just because we are and that his motives are always to rescue us from the law, then we can enter into a life-changing depth of intimacy where listening turns to hearing and seeing turns to vision.

## THE EARS OF AN INTIMATE

Everything has a sound. I recently heard Stevie Wonder, the musical superstar, say that he sees with sound. It's no secret that Stevie is blind and has been since birth. But his statement really impacted me, because I have often had to let the sound of God's voice direct me when I could not see where I was headed.

I'm reminded of a trip our family took to the Carlsbad Caverns in New Mexico, a site referred to as "the darkest place on earth." For a short while, the guide turns off his flashlight and directs your steps with the sound of his voice. You are actually seeing with sound. Of course, for safety reasons, we also had the security of a rope to hold on to, but it was his voice that we followed. The darkness was indescribable, and yet we could discern whether he was moving to the right or the left by his spoken word.

Perhaps you will relate as I confess that there have been times in my life when God's will seemed as dark to me as the Carlsbad Caverns. The good news, however, is that during those same times I learned to press in to my loving heavenly Father to hear his voice. The written Word became my rope, and I just kept on reading until one day it came alive. It was as if God was actually speaking aloud into the darkness of my situation, and the choices I made were finally based on where his voice directed. I didn't hear correctly every time, and sometimes I still make mistakes in hearing, but I have used his written Word as the plumb line to get me back on course.

And not to burst any bubbles here, but I'm convinced that nobody, and I do mean nobody, hears God correctly all the time. If that were possible, we would not need faith, humility, and patience—all of which are necessary to cultivate godly character.

Instead, we learn to hear God by holding on to his written Word in anticipation of its becoming an inner road map speaking into our darkness. Psalm 119:105 reiterates my point: "Your word is a lamp to my feet and a light to my path" (NASB). Will there be dull times? Absolutely. Will there be times when we would rather dash out of the cave and go by sight? Of course! But we learn to hear by obeying the written Word until suddenly both God's written and spoken words are directing our paths.

In the process, we find ourselves making the choice to become either listeners or hearers. Listeners are those who hear the Word, remember the Word, and maybe even teach the Word—but they don't live it! On the other hand, hearers are those who let the Word prompt them into action. The Word takes root and their lives bear the fruit of it.

And so we reap what we sow. Listen to God's statement in Zechariah 7:13: "When I called, they did not listen; so when they called, I would not listen." As in any relationship, we can only put God off so many times before the communication breaks down completely.

When my kids were little, I would say, "Did you hear me?" Clearly, they knew I wasn't talking about words; I was talking about action. Real hearing always touches the heart and summons a call to action. At times I've hurt so deeply I wondered how I would survive it. Inevitably, some well-meaning person would listen to my plight and start telling me how to handle it. By contrast, I've also had some amazing hearers come alongside to weep with me, hug me, and let me be undone without trying to *fix* my feelings. These are the ones who responded by bringing a meal, or watching my kids, or just giving me some of their time to let me talk. They heard; they became my intimates.

Real hearing means that we, just as the Good Samaritan in Luke 10, respond to others as if it were God's need that we are meeting. Prayer is just listening if it does not result in action. God has no voice, no hands, no feet, and no provision to use but ours.

The following story, told brilliantly by Tim Hansel, illustrates the difference between those who listen and those who hear for God's sake:

> *A seminary professor . . . scheduled his students to preach on the Parable of the Good Samaritan. . . . Each student, one at a time, had to walk down a certain corridor and pass by a bum, who was deliberately planted there, obviously in need of some sort of aid. . . .*
>
> *The percentage of those good men and women who stopped to help was extremely low; especially for those who were under the pressure of a shorter time period. . . . Rushing to preach a sermon on the Good Samaritan, they had walked past the beggar at the heart of the parable. . . . The following powerful poem expresses it best:*

>> *I was hungry and you formed a humanities club to discuss my hunger.*
>> *Thank you.*
>> *I was imprisoned and you crept off quietly to your chapel to pray for my release.*
>> *Nice.*
>> *I was naked and in your mind you debated the morality of my appearance.*
>> *What good did that do?*

*I was sick and you knelt and thanked God for your health.*
*But I needed you.*
*I was homeless and you preached to me of the shelter of the*
     *love of God.*
*I wish you'd taken me home.*
*I was lonely and you left me alone to pray for me.*
*Why didn't you stay?*
*You seem so holy, so close to God; but I'm still very hungry,*
     *lonely, cold, and still in pain.*
*Does it matter?*[3]

Indeed it does matter, because hearers are those who receive vision.

## THE EYES OF INTIMACY

Years ago I was listening to a Christian talk-radio show when a man telephoned the program from his hospital room. He had used a fire poker to gouge out his own eye after reading, "If your eye causes you to sin, pluck it out" (Mark 9:47). I was horrified! That poor man saw the words with his physical eyes but did not have the vision of an intimate to understand them. If only he had seen the real meaning: "If the way you are looking at things is causing you to sin, pluck out the way you look at them. Get God's vision."

What we take in with our physical eyes is called "sight," but what we take in through a heart connection to God is "insight." Insight is always the basis for vision. Sight is looking at things as they are, whereas vision is seeing what things can be.

When Michelangelo saw a piece of marble, he looked beyond a white piece of rock and carved out what it could be. God's Word says, "Where there is no vision, the people perish" (Prov.

29:18 KJV). In other words, when we live by what we see physically rather than according to what God imagines for others, or ourselves, or the things around us, we are robbed of life.

When you and I develop an intimate connection with Jesus, then he will add vision to the way we see him. The Old Testament uses four Hebrew words for "vision." The first one is *chazah*, meaning to mentally perceive, contemplate (with pleasure); specifically to have a vision of: to behold, look, and prophesy.

During a recent trip to Spokane, Washington, a friend took me to see a botanical garden. As we sat observing the different flowers, I realized the considerable amount of time gardeners had invested in tending and cultivating such beauty. Soon my observation changed to a gaze.

As an observer, I was on a fact-finding mission, asking questions about what I saw in the natural: "What is the name of this plant?" or "How often does this plant flower?" Observation questions address what is. However, a gaze is a deeper look that eventually leads to vision. A gaze is more like absorbing than observing. At the garden, I gazed at the heavenly display of God's handiwork. Captivated by the variety of vibrant colors and unusual shapes of flowers, I soon forgot about myself and got lost in the immensity, intensity, and creativity of our Creator.

When I returned to my hotel room, the Holy Spirit spoke to me about the fact that I had been at the garden not to pick a flower, not to determine its origin, and not to get something from it. My purpose was to gaze, to meditate, to perceive, and in the process develop new vision. Such is the case with intimacy. As we gaze upon Jesus, we will perceive our heavenly Bridegroom with new vision. No longer will it be about you or me; we will be lost in Jesus, the Rose of Sharon. He knows full well that we are all prone to wander, to lose vision of the prize. But the more we gaze, the less we will want to look elsewhere.

The second word for "vision" is *chizzâyôn*, meaning a revelation, especially by dream. Several of my friends dream almost
every night—and not just short dreams—they're in full-blown
Technicolor cinematography. I also know of people who seldom
dream; however, when they do, they're acutely aware that God
might be revealing something important.

I recommend that you record your dreams. Try hard to
remember every imaginable detail, including the date for future
verification. Take note of the people involved. Who are they?
What role do they play in your life? It might be what or whom
that person represents that God wants you to notice. Dreams
often contain symbolism that may offer great revelation. For
example, a young man I know rented a room to someone from
his church. Shortly thereafter, he had a dream that his renter
was sitting in his room with a loaded gun in his hand. God used
a dream to alert my friend to danger. When the renter chose
to move, this man was relieved to let him go. John (not his real
name) never knew for sure if the renter was a danger to him,
but when the renter moved his belongings from the apartment,
John experienced peace again.

We've talked about dreams in an earlier chapter, but I want
to reiterate that if you learn to watch for symbolism, you will
find that God can use the revelation in your dreams to increase
vision.

There's also another type of *chizzâyôn* vision: daydreaming.
As a child you may have been chastised for daydreaming (which
means you are probably an artist of some sort), but dreaming to
have a more intimate love for Jesus is admirable.

The third Hebrew word for "vision" is *mareh*, meaning to
view in the visible realm. The primary role of an intercessor
is to be a watchman on the wall who will pray, "Thy kingdom
come, Thy will be done in earth, as it is in heaven" (Matt. 6:10
KJV). Twenty-four times Jesus tells us to watch.

During the first Persian Gulf War, Americans would watch on TV with amazement the new technology of infrared thermal night vision. This equipment included a unique helmet that allowed our military to see in the dark for the purpose of honing in to hit the target. Similarly, as we grow in intimacy, our infrared night vision will develop with supernatural eyes to see what Jesus sees, feel what he feels, and act on behalf of his purposes.

Our fourth Hebrew word for "vision" is *marah*, meaning to gaze into a mirror or looking glass. James 1:23–24 says, "Anyone who listens to the word but does not do what it says is like a man who looks at his face in a mirror and, after looking at himself, goes away and immediately forgets what he looks like."

The more we gaze into the mirror of God's Word, the more we will see Jesus reflected in our lives. He will give us vision to see in ourselves the potential for all that we can be.

For example, God called Nehemiah to rebuild the walls of Jerusalem, a daunting task that the most skilled of men would find challenging. Tobiah the Ammonite and Sanballat the Samarian were Israel's adversaries. In Nehemiah 4:2–3 Tobiah and Sanballat said, "What are those feeble Jews doing? Will they restore their wall? Will they offer sacrifices? Will they finish in a day? Can they bring the stones back to life from those heaps of rubble—burned as they are? . . . What they are building—if even a fox climbed up on it, he would break down their wall of stones!" Cleverly, God used these enemies to challenge Nehemiah and help build his confidence in God to continue building the wall, for Nehemiah prayed, "O God, strengthen my hands" (6:9 KJV).

Our enemy uses the same strategy today. He says, "Who are you? You are so weak and feeble. God doesn't hear your prayers," or "You don't deserve to be close to Jesus." Yet we have God's

Word to gaze upon, to look into as a mirror that will reflect what he envisioned when he created us.

In closing, the following words from Dr. P. P. Bliss express it all: "Wonderful things in the Bible I see. This is the dearest, that Jesus loves me." When you hear and see and know that you are loved, you will be compelled to act on it.

# CHAPTER 10

# The Oneness of Intimacy

*There's a wonderful story about Jimmy Durante, one of the great entertainers of a generation ago. He was asked to be a part of a show for World War II veterans. He told them his schedule was very busy and he could afford only a few minutes, but if they wouldn't mind his doing one short monologue and immediately leaving for his next appointment, he would come. Of course, the show's director agreed happily. But when Jimmy got on stage, something interesting happened. He went through the short mono-logue and then stayed. The applause grew louder and louder and he kept staying. Pretty soon, he had been on fifteen, twenty, then thirty minutes. Finally he took a last bow and left the stage. Backstage someone stopped him and said, "I thought you had to go after a few minutes. What happened?"*

*Jimmy answered, "I did have to go, but I can show you the reason I stayed. You can see for yourself if you'll look down on the front row." In the front row were two men,*

*each of whom had lost an arm in the war. One had lost his
right arm and the other had lost his left. Together, they
were able to clap, and that's exactly what they were doing,
loudly and cheerfully.[1]*

These two men remind me of the way our oneness works
in Christ. We can't accomplish our purpose without him, and
he can't accomplish his plan for a spiritual family without us. I
like the way Dutch Sheets explains God's interdependence with
us in his timeless classic *Intercessory Prayer*: "God chose, from
the time of the Creation, to work on the earth *through* humans,
not independent of them. He always has and always will, even
at the cost of becoming one. Though God is sovereign and all-
powerful, Scripture clearly tells us that He limited Himself,
concerning the affairs of earth, to working through human
beings."[2] That's trust. That's love.

Like the two men in the Durante story, Jesus is at the
right hand of God in heaven, and we are his hands here on
earth. Together, nothing is impossible. Together, John 15:5
assures us, we will bear much fruit. That's the beauty of being
his bride.

## PREPARED TO MULTIPLY

There's something refreshing about being around a newly
married couple. They're so focused on each other, so eager to
touch one another, so anxious to be alone. You just know that
their union will multiply into another branch of life. And so it
is with Jesus.

As we spend time in his presence, intimacy will give birth
to prayers for others, and his ability to father through us will
become evident. It's during those intimate times alone with

him that he touches the private things in our lives that will eventually cause us to multiply.

Not to alarm you, but hidden agendas will be exposed and deceptions in the heart will be lovingly stripped away. The Lover of your soul will begin to take off the things that need to be removed from your heart to bring you into greater intimacy, and he will do it progressively.

As a young Christian, I remember thinking that if I could do great things for God, I would be a success. Now after decades of loving him, I have discovered that it's not the size of my work but the size of my love for him that matters. When we leave this earth, our time here will not be measured by the greatness of our work, but rather by the greatness of our love for the Lord and others. The reason I long to go to heaven is not to escape hell, but to experience God forever.

The purpose of our bride and bridegroom relationship is that we might know him in a purity and depth that we can't experience with another. Jesus said, "Blessed are the pure in heart, for they will see God" (Matt. 5:8). According to Jesus, intimacy is contingent upon our willingness to have our hearts purified.

None of us can say that we are spotless, or without blemish, because the biggest giant you or I face is the one staring back at us in the mirror. We are constantly tempted to lift "self" up, but we must say no to the prideful ambitions of life. Purity is a moment-by-moment choice to yield our selfish desires to the Lord for the sake of giving him a spiritual family.

I once saw a skit in which a man climbed into a casket and closed his eyes, insisting that he was dead to self. Minutes later, he crawled out and stood before the audience, active as ever. That's the way the flesh is. It must be starved to death, starved until it no longer has the strength to demand its own way.

Our heavenly husband wants us to be secure in his love, not in self. The reason: so that we will lay down our lives to reproduce secure, godly children. I'm sure we've all met insecure leaders who are more concerned about making themselves look great than about bringing others forward. And yet can you imagine a loving parent or teacher who did not want to see the child or student grow greater than himself? Jesus emphasized this point in the way he lived: "Anyone who has faith in me will do what I have been doing. He will do *even greater things* than these, because I am going to the Father" (John 14:12, emphasis added). He loved through sacrifice, washing the feet of others, and laying down his own life to lift us up. He demonstrated pure love.

The more our love has been purified, the more we are able to lay our lives down, regardless of the cost to self. Perhaps you have seen a movie called *The End of the Spear*. It's the true story of five missionaries who traveled into the Amazon jungle in search of the Waodani, a fierce tribe that was destroying itself through selfishness, lies, and murder. After finally making contact, these five faithful missionaries were fatally speared by the tribesmen. During the attack, they refused to fight back and instead offered the love of Christ. So great was the impact of their love that the Waodani chief and the man responsible for the killing eventually embraced the families of these missionaries and surrendered their lives to Christ.

At one point, the Waodani who led the attack took a missionary's son to the place where he had killed his father. As was the custom of a life for a life, he handed over his spear and instructed the missionary's son to kill him. I'll never forget the son's response, "You didn't take my father's life; he laid it down for you." Love lays down the right to self, no matter what the cost. Jesus said, "Whoever wants to save his life will lose it" (Mark 8:35).

Whether we are put on a shelf, persecuted, or used for something great—if we love, we lay down our right to self in order to find life in Christ. When our hearts have been purified through death to self, hindrances are small things, temporary things— things to be laid down for the One we love.

Then, when it is no longer God *and* me but Christ *in* me, we are prepared to bear fruit. Intimacy is about bringing others forth. Launching others into an abundant life. Birthing them into the greatness of their heavenly father. But to prepare for the delivery room, we must starve the things that make us selfish, jealous, and self-serving and instead feed on the love of God to grow in his likeness.

This might be a good time to address an issue that often cripples the child of God: *feelings.* Let me state right here and now that you don't feel your way into intimacy, you surrender your way there. Feelings are what the enemy places at the end of his spear to kill your relationship with God and others. If you try to feel your way into holiness, you will end up a defeated, bitter Christian.

Mature Christians are those who touch others, but they are not touchy. I once knew a woman called to do great feats for God, but regrettably her feelings were easily hurt and she refused to address her issues. Her full potential was never realized because she allowed feelings to rule her heart. Everyone loses when we refuse to surrender to God. Those who could have received through us are robbed, and we who need to grow are limited in our ability to do so. How sad.

Before Jesus ascended to heaven, he gave us one Great Commission: "Go into all the world and preach the good news to all creation" (Mark 16:15). The reason our part in this mission has not been fulfilled is that our hearts have not been purified enough to see God. And we certainly can't show others what we haven't seen ourselves.

## GETTING ON THE POTTER'S WHEEL

The world is looking for the signs, wonders, and miracles that Jesus said would follow those who believe. So why aren't we seeing them? Because we refuse to get on the potter's wheel and let God mold us into a vessel fit for his use. We don't want to be re-made; we want to be self-made. Most Christians have been so busy working for the Kingdom that we have avoided the touch of the King.

George Müller, Mother Teresa, Corrie ten Boom, and Smith Wigglesworth had one thing in common: they were so emptied of self that God had plenty of room to pour his power through them. The power of love took them to the potter's wheel, not once—but daily. You've probably heard that one *week* without prayer makes one a *weak* Christian. If we don't spend time worshiping the Master Potter (God), we will focus on ourselves, the clay. Without time in the Lord's presence, we tend to become pleasant-looking, powerless Christians with nothing to offer the world but our own strength.

When we surrender our lives to the potter, God's power works in and through us. We have become one with him in purpose, and we'll give birth to his fruit in our lives. Whatever we give birth to will look like the one with whom we have had intimacy. The Master Potter's child will look like an intimate used for the purposes of God. When God's pure love has touched our inward parts, we will know his power, show his power, and birth a powerful group of intimates for him.

## BECOMING ONE WITH OTHERS

There's been a lot of discussion about what Jesus meant when he prayed, "that they all may be one, as You, Father, are in Me, and I in You; that they also may be one in Us, that the world may believe that You sent Me" (John 17:21 NKJV). This verse conjures up in my mind a picture of family.

No matter how dysfunctional a family might be, or how much they might disagree among themselves, an outsider soon learns that no one on the outside messes with family. They belong to each other. Generally speaking, they have certain things in common: their blood, their name, their relatives, their commitment, their beliefs, and their inheritance. Though personalities and physical looks vary greatly, it's what they share that makes them one.

I'm blessed to come from a family where we all enjoy each other's company. But you don't have to *like* your relatives to *love* them. To like means you're happy about spending time together. But to love is to desire the ultimate good for another, no matter how much you dislike his or her personality.

Whether a biological family or God's family, certain commonalities do unite us and ought to motivate us to desire the ultimate good for others. In fact, Jesus said that our unity and love for one another are the very things that will cause the unbelieving world to seek him and want to become part of his family.

Today, with so much divorce and so many fatherless homes, people are looking for family. They are looking for the heavenly Father, the One who will never leave them or forsake them. They are looking for a place to belong. What they're not looking for is a bunch of relatives who fight, backbite, and reject each other. Heaven forbid! We all want a home where we can experience peace.

The apostle Paul said, "If it is possible, as far as it depends on you, live at peace with everyone" (Rom. 12:18). And how do we do that? We prefer one another. I give you the bigger piece of the pie, or open the door for you to enter first. I give you the honor, because in doing so I honor the Lord. Jesus said that whatever you or I do to the least of his people, we have done to him. When people see our actions, they should want to know more about Jesus.

Unfortunately, all too often when people fall into sin, they are judged and rejected by the church. Many never return. But Paul said, "If someone is caught in a sin, you who are spiritual should restore him gently. But watch yourself, or you also may be tempted. Carry each other's burdens, and in this way you will fulfill the law of Christ" (Gal. 6:1–2).

Christ doesn't discard people who fail and admit it; he offers them hope and dignity. When a repentant man or woman has to face the devastating consequences of his or her actions, that person needs support both spiritually and emotionally in order to be fully restored.

One of Eddie's main callings is to father and restore fallen leaders. He doesn't skirt issues, but rather he helps them to talk through their fear, anger, and shame. We recently met with a popular pastor and his wife who were removed from ministry because he had broken his marriage vows by having an affair. Eddie had spoken in his church some years back and stayed in contact on a limited basis. His church had been quite celebrated in certain circles of their denomination.

When we met with this couple, the husband was completely broken, repentant, and desperately longing to mend his marriage. He confessed that he had felt trapped in deception and didn't know how to get out. He also said that he had no one to turn to for help. Meanwhile, the church had abandoned him and his family. They were left high and dry with no financial or emotional support. Instead of offering prayer and counsel, the people they had served offered them only disdain. Dishonor turned to disgrace, and he went from the darling to the damned in his congregation.

Let's talk straight here. We certainly don't condone sin, and we do believe that fallen pastors should step down from leadership positions. However, they also need to receive hope and encouragement in order to be restored. Many Christians are quick to judge those who fall into sexual sins, but what about the "respectable" sins that seldom receive mention? Anything that we do to deliberately hurt, dishonor, or misrepresent another person is something that reflects a lack of integrity of heart.

The Lord does not turn a blind eye to any sin. However, he is about justice, not merely vengeance, which is why he paid a price for our sins that we were incapable of paying. So if we *really* understood what Christ did for us, we would never want anything but mercy for others. Only when we truly see our own wretchedness will we want to extend grace to the best and the worst of others.

Perhaps one reason God called David a man after his own heart is that he was determined to put the desires of God and others above his own. He didn't care about positioning before people; he cared about pleasing God. By maintaining that posture, he treated everyone else like a king and eventually sat on the throne himself.

Before we can see God, we need to see ourselves in our fellowman.

We are the same as everyone else who has failed—we simply fail differently. The human race ought not be about competition, but rather a race to the foot of the cross, for it is there that we are made one with Christ and one with each other.

I'd like to share a poem that brings the struggle of our journey into perspective. It's a Christian takeoff on Rudyard Kipling's poem "If."

# If

*If you can trust when everyone about you*
 *Is doubting Him, proclaiming Him untrue;*
*If you can hope in Christ, tho' all forsake you*
 *And say 'tis not the thing for you to do;*

*If you can wait on God, nor wish to hurry,*
 *Or, being greatly used, keep humble still;*
*Or if you're tested, still refuse to worry,*
 *And so remain within His sovereign will;*

*If you can say, 'tis well, when sorrow greets you,*
 *And death has taken those you hold most dear;*
*If you can smile when adverse trials meet you,*
 *And be content e'en tho' your lot be drear;*

*If you can be reviled and never murmur,*
 *Or being tempted, not give way to sin;*
*If you fight for right and stand the firmer,*
 *Or lose the battle when you ought to win—*

*If you can really long for His appearing,*
 *And therefore set your heart on things above;*
*If you can speak for Christ in spite of sneering,*
 *Or to the most unlovely one show love;*

*If you can hear the call of God to labour,*
 *And answer, "Yes" in yieldedness and trust,*
*And go to tell the story of the Savior*
 *To souls in darkness o'er the desert dust;*

*If you can pray when Satan's darts are strongest,*
  *And take the road of faith instead of sight;*
*Or walk with God, e'en tho' His way be longest,*
  *And swerve not to the left nor to the right;*

*If you desire Himself alone to fill you,*
  *For Him alone you care to live and be;*
*Then 'tis not you, but CHRIST Who dwelleth in you,*
  *And that, O child of God, is victory.*[3]

# CHAPTER 11

# Ten Virgins and Two Brides

Married sixty-three years with their ups and downs, Benjamin and Hulda Edwards were still devoted to each other when he died at eighty-six. Even more so, they were devoted to God. He had been a singer, director, and the composer of hundreds of sacred hymns.

Years after Benjamin's passing, my friend Karen Kaufman met Hulda Edwards at a Bible study. She was ninety-eight years old and in the throes of dementia. But here was a woman who had so exhibited love for God, love for his Word, and love for his people that it flowed out of her like water from an open tap. Walking down the hall at the assisted living residence on her way to the powder room, Karen said she would pass Hulda's room and see her lying in bed quoting Scripture and talking to God as if he was sitting by her bedside.

Now and then Hulda would join the ladies for Bible study and astound them with one of her nuggets of wisdom. On one such occasion, Karen remembers: "We were talking about character and how important it is to encourage others with compliments. I didn't think Hulda was paying any attention at all when she suddenly piped in with, 'Yes, but if you compliment a

135

man who is unworthy, you will only make him more of what he already is.' The words washed over me with such power that I never wanted to flatter an undeserving man or woman again."

Friend, God desires that all of us have an overflow of relationship with him—just the kind that Hulda experienced. Then, no matter what happens to our minds, the words that pour out of our mouths will reflect the fullness of his presence in our hearts.

## TEN VIRGINS

There's been much disagreement among Christians over whether or not you can lose your salvation. Personally, I think they're asking the wrong question. It's not "Will God ever leave you?" (And by the way, the answer is no. Remember, the Lord promised in Hebrews 13:5, "Never will I leave you; never will I forsake you.") The real question is "Will you forsake him?"

Consider the story of the ten virgins in Matthew 25. In fact, let's read it in context so there is no misunderstanding:

> *The kingdom of heaven will be like ten virgins who took their lamps and went out to meet the bridegroom. Five of them were foolish and five were wise. The foolish ones took their lamps but did not take any oil with them. The wise, however, took oil in jars along with their lamps. The bridegroom was a long time in coming, and they all became drowsy and fell asleep. At midnight the cry rang out: "Here's the bridegroom! Come out to meet him!" Then all the virgins woke up and trimmed their lamps. The foolish ones said to the wise, "Give us some of your oil; our lamps are going out." "No," they replied, "there may not be enough for both us and you. Instead, go to those who sell oil*

*and buy some for yourselves." But while they were on their*
*way to buy the oil, the bridegroom arrived. The virgins*
*who were ready went in with him to the wedding banquet.*
*And the door was shut. Later the others also came. "Sir!*
*Sir!" they said. "Open the door for us!" But he replied, "I*
*tell you the truth, I don't know you"* (vv. 1–12).

The story of the ten virgins is about maintaining intimacy. The ten virgins represent the professing Christian church, those who claim to have been purified by Jesus. This passage infers that they all began with some oil. So let's start by talking about oil. There are two kinds: First, natural oil, which represents worldly power. Second, spiritual oil, which represents the anointing of the Holy Spirit.

*In Leviticus 14:17 oil was applied to the ear so that hear-*
*ing would be entirely God-ward and for the Word of God.*
*It was applied to the thumb for the work of the priest was*
*to be for God in the power of the Holy Spirit. It was to*
*be applied to the toe for his walk was to be with God and*
*before God, walking in the Holy Spirit.*[1]

The oil that the ten virgins required for their lamps represents the power, or intimacy, needed to maintain our relationship with the Lord. Our lamp represents the way we see God; our oil is the way we walk out our intimacy. Our oil is our closeness; it's the fuel of our relationship.

Whether you come from an established spiritual heritage or none at all, you and I must choose to keep our relationship with the Lord current and intimate, just as the five wise virgins did. It doesn't matter how close your friends or family are to the Lord, it matters how close you are. None of us can borrow another Christian's relationship with God.

As we've already established earlier in this book, intimacy with the Lord is not a commodity that can be purchased through works, or friends, or great achievements as the five foolish virgins hoped to do. They went to buy the oil because they had not carried it in their hearts. But you can't buy love; you can only maintain the love already extended to you.

These five foolish virgins demonstrate to us that what we don't cherish, we don't invest in. They refused to spend time in preparation. And even when it came down to the wire, they walked away hoping to purchase what they could have had all along.

The foolish virgins began in the right place, but they became lazy about the part that no one sees. Eventually that laziness led them away from the bridegroom. I believe it was Spurgeon who said, "It is better to be one step away from hell with your feet headed toward heaven than it is to be one step away from heaven headed toward hell." Compromise begins small, but it can take us further away than we expected to go and cost us far more than we ever intended to pay.

No matter where we are today, we can increase our oil. We can start to spend time alone with Jesus and then decide to maintain that intimacy on a daily basis. You and I can't live on yesterday's relationship. Like the Israelites in the wilderness, we must go after fresh spiritual bread every day.

If we stay current with the Lord, our lamps will stay bright, and we will have extra oil for those times when the road of life is dark and rough. We will also have enough to light the path and leave a footprint for others to see. As Moses said about Asher: "May he be esteemed by his brothers; may he bathe his feet in olive oil" (Deut. 33:24 NLT).

"The oil represents a smooth, fragrant and delightful walk in the Spirit by this great man of God. An impression would be left behind at each step. So the Spirit-filled man leaves behind him fragrant impressions of his walk with the Lord in the Spirit."[2]

There's a great story about our fragrance in *The Lay-Driven Church*: A prominent Bible teacher was invited to give a series of lectures. At each gathering, he noticed a delightful, flower-like fragrance permeating the room. After the second evening, he asked the pastor where the delightful aroma came from. The pastor explained that a few people who worked at the perfume factory had to come directly from their work to the meetings. Unknown to them, their clothes, having absorbed the fragrance of their environment, were releasing it into the room.[3] Likewise, as we spend time in God's presence, we will not only become a sweet-smelling aroma to the Lord, but the world we live in will be changed too. The five foolish virgins knew who had the oil. They could see it; they could smell it, but they disregarded the treasure given them.

## Two Kinds of Brides

The Lord has two kinds of brides: the faithful and the unfaithful, the *giving* and the *give-me*. We all vacillate between the two. The faithful or giving bride, much like Mother Teresa, sees the whole world as a family that she can serve. The unfaithful or give-me bride sees the whole world as a family to serve her needs.

Listen to this account of an encounter with Mother Teresa. A very wealthy man went to meet with her because he had heard how she cared for and held in her arms the poorest of the dying poor in the streets of Calcutta. He had heard how she slept in the chicken coop in order to make room for the sick. Finally in her presence, the wealthy man said, "I wouldn't do what you do for a million dollars." And she replied, "Neither would I!"

She did it for Christ.

On the other hand, there was Elisha's servant Gehazi, who chased after the world. His story is told in 2 Kings 5. Elisha had healed Naaman, a military commander, of leprosy and told him about the living God. And Naaman was so grateful that he offered riches and clothing in return. But Elisha refused it. Later, however, Gehazi pursued Naaman and crafted a lie about needing the money for Elisha's benefit. Naaman gladly gave it, and Gehazi believed that he had succeeded in his deception. Sadly, the leprosy that was removed from Naaman was placed on Gehazi, and years later he was walking in the shadows with nothing but memories of God's power in his life.

Gehazi, like the unfaithful or give-me bride, sought after something temporary and lost focus on the eternal. He had lived and served with one of the greatest prophets of all time, yet his heart was so full of greed that he did not realize what he had lost.

I believe that everyone who comes to Christ has intermittent struggles with being unfaithful or having a give-me attitude. Surely not everyone is tempted by materialism, or recognition, or lust. Some of us, like the five foolish virgins, struggle instead with time. We know that life is time, and yet we want to use it for ourselves and not for God's purposes.

Jesus' call to every believer is to go into the world and make disciples. And there are many ways to do so. We can go ourselves, send out missionaries, send our resources, and above all, we can send our prayers.

The Bible says, "Very early in the morning, while it was still dark, Jesus got up, left the house and went off to a solitary place, where he prayed" (Mark 1:35). He went up to pray so that he could bring down the miracles.

The first miracle Jesus ever performed was at a wedding, but he used people to do it. John says in chapter 2 that the wine ran out during the wedding festivities so Jesus' mother told the servants, "Do whatever he tells you" (v. 5). The servants were the ones who filled the jars with water; they were the ones who poured it out and watched it turn to wine.

Often, we miss the supernatural by refusing to do the natural. We look for big things to do for God and forget that greatness comes from being faithful in the little things. But there is still time to change.

Today, we can be part of his miracles by filling our mornings with prayer and pouring ourselves out for others. I remember one morning during a time of intercession when the Lord said, "Alice, it's as if my bride has had an epidural in her back. [An epidural is a regional anesthesia that numbs the body during childbirth.] She's numb from the waist down. The spiritual baby is in the birth canal, but my bride isn't pushing because she's numb and doesn't realize how near the baby is to birth. My bride, my bride [the church], she can't feel the birth pains. She's busy with her life, but I want to give her so much more. My bride isn't pushing in prayer for new souls to be born into my Kingdom. It's time to push for the end-times revival. She doesn't know how to weep and cry out in prayer . . . she's numb. If only she would push for my will to be done on earth!"

When you and I realize the importance of our part in prayer, we will pray. We will push. We will do the next thing Jesus tells us to do. And then, when the door finally closes at the wedding banquet in heaven, we will be like those five wise virgins who had more than enough oil because they invested love and intimacy in the heavenly Bridegroom.

## Renewing Your Vows

I started this book with a wedding and I will end it with one. However, this story will be quite different from that of the unfaithful bride you read about earlier in this chapter. This love story is really about you. But before we get there, let me share a personal experience.

Two years ago our youngest daughter Ashlee married, and we invested months of preparation time on every detail for her special day. The country club was just across the street from our church, so we booked a sit-down dinner reception for the attendees and our newlywed couple. The ice sculpture of Ashlee and Chris glistened in the dining hall of the ballroom. We had chosen special napkins, gorgeous wedding and groom's cakes, engraved invitations, and just the right flowers—it was such a fun and a special time!

The wedding was exquisite. Ashlee was gorgeous. And Chris Morris, her future husband, was clearly nervous—even though he was deliriously handsome with his tall slim physique, crew-cut hair, and light blue eyes.

Five bridesmaids made their way down the church aisle, and then the wedding march began. As the music swelled, the doors swung open and there she was dressed in pure white with a huge smile stretched across her face. She glowed with joy and excitement. Ashlee's gown flowed gracefully as her proud dad, Eddie, walked her down the aisle toward Chris.

I tried not to cry, but I wasn't very successful. Our family and friends stood in honor of our daughter's love covenant as she stepped slowly toward her new future. At the end of the vows, when Mr. and Mrs. Chris Morris turned to face the crowd, they began walking hand in hand. Two lives joined as one. Their dream had come true. Joy and celebration filled their hearts and permeated the church that evening.

All of us love wedding stories. Now it's your turn. Will you walk with Jesus hand in hand? So why not let me celebrate with you as you renew your wedding vows with him?

That's right. Stand to your feet, bride of Christ, and let Jesus clasp your hands. His hands are strong enough to pull you out of all your hardships, hurts, and failures. His hands are gentle enough to soothe your fears, lead you toward a new future, and wipe away all your tears. Yes, his hands are splintered and scarred from the cross he carried for you, but they are also firm and reassuring. His hands will always be there for you.

Jesus has committed to never leave you nor forsake you (Heb. 13:5). You are his bride. He longs for a deep and fulfilling relationship with you.

Now with a calm and deep sense of commitment flowing through your soul, slowly and deliberately read aloud your vow to Jesus. Once you have done so, read aloud what the Lord Jesus, your heavenly Groom, pledges to you.

## YOUR VOW TO JESUS:

I, <your name>, take you, Jesus, to be my heavenly wedded husband. To have and to hold from this day forward. I pledge before God and these witnesses (heavenly witnesses) to be your loving and faithful bride. Jesus, I will love and honor you, cherish and obey you, and forsaking all others, I will keep myself totally for you. In plenty and in want, in joy and in sorrow, in sickness and in health, through adversity or suffering, I will trust you. I give my whole heart to you, Lord, in token and pledge of my constant faith and abiding love.

## JESUS' VOW TO YOU:

I, Jesus, choose you, <your name>, to be my wedded bride. To have and to hold you forever. I formed you in your mother's womb and called you out of darkness. I bought you with my life, and I have fulfilled the law for you. I am preparing a place for you, that where I am, you may be also. I will never leave you or forsake you. Call unto me and I will answer you. I will always be a shield about you. I have given you my name and all authority to use it. You are my beloved. My blood I give for you, in token and pledge of my constant devotion to you.

Now that you are married to the Lover of your soul, dare to meet Jesus in the bridal chamber of your heart. Let me be the first to say—Congratulations!!!

# Suggested Reading

Alves, Elizabeth. *Becoming a Prayer Warrior.* Ventura, CA: Regal Books, 1998.

Bickle, Mike. *Passion for Jesus.* Orlando, FL: Creation House, 1993.

Billheimer, Paul E. *Destined for the Throne.* Fort Washington, PA: Christian Literature Crusade, 1975.

Dawson, Joy. *Intimate Friendship with God.* Grand Rapids, MI: Chosen Books, 1986.

Deere, Jack. *Surprised by the Power of the Spirit.* Grand Rapids, MI: Zondervan Publishing House, 1993.

Eastman, Dick. *Beyond Imagination.* Grand Rapids, MI: Chosen Books, 1997.

———. *The Jericho Hour.* Altamonte Springs, FL: Creation House, 1994.

———. *Love on Its Knees.* Grand Rapids, MI: Fleming H. Revell Co., 1989.

Edwards, Gene. *A Tale of Three Kings*. Wheaton, IL: Tyndale House Publishers, 1992.

Frangipane, Francis. *The House of the Lord*. Lake Mary, FL: Creation House, 1991.

Grubb, Norman. *Rees Howells, Intercessor.* Fort Washington, PA: Christian Literature Crusade, 1962.

Guyon, Jeanne. *Experiencing the Depths of Jesus Christ*. Gardiner, ME: Christian Books, 1981.

Hamon, Bill. *Prophets and Personal Prophecy*. Shippensburg, PA: Destiny Image Publishers, 1987.

Hinn, Benny. *Welcome, Holy Spirit*. Milton Keynes, England: Word Publishing, 1995.

Hinn, Sam. *Kissing the Face of God*. Lake Mary, FL: Charisma House, 2002.

Jacobs, Cindy. *Possessing the Gates of the Enemy*. Grand Rapids, MI: Chosen Books, 1991.

———. *The Voice of God*. Ventura, CA: Regal Books, 1995.

Law, Terry. *The Power of Praise and Worship*. Tulsa, OK: Victory House Publishers, 1985.

Marshall, Catherine. *Something More*. New York, NY: Avon Books, 1976.

Murray, Andrew. *The Ministry of Intercession*. Springdale, PA: Whitaker House, 1982.

Nee, Watchman. *Spiritual Authority*. Richmond, VA: Christian Fellowship Publisher, 1972.

———. *The Release of the Spirit*. Cloverdale, IN: Sure Foundation Publishers, 1965.

Penn-Lewis, Jessie. *Life Out of Death*. Parkstone, England.

Prince, Derek. *Shaping History Through Prayer and Fasting*. Fort Lauderdale, FL: Derek Prince Ministries, 1973.

Shankle, Randy. *The Merismos*. Marshall, TX: Christian Publishing Services, Inc., 1987.

Sheets, Dutch. *Intercessory Prayer*. Ventura, CA: Regal Books, 1996.

Sherrer, Quin, and Ruthanne Garlock. *A Woman's Guide to Breaking Bondages*. Ann Arbor, MI: Servant Publications, 1994.

———. *The Spiritual Warrior's Prayer Guide*. Ann Arbor, MI: Servant Publications, 1992.

Sjoberg, Kjell. *Winning the Prayer War*. Chichester, England: New Wine Press, 1991.

Smith, Alice. *Beyond the Lie*. Minneapolis, MN: Bethany House, 2006.

———. *Beyond the Veil*. Ventura, CA: Regal Books, 1996.

———. *Delivering the Captives*. Minneapolis, MN: Bethany House, 2007.

Smith, Eddie. *Breaking the Enemy's Grip*. Minneapolis, MN: Bethany House, 2005.

———. *How to Be Heard in Heaven*. Minneapolis, MN: Bethany House, 2007.

Tozer, A.W. *The Knowledge of the Holy*. San Francisco, CA: Harper & Row Publishers, 1961.

Wagner, C. Peter. *Prayer Shield*. Ventura, CA: Regal Books, 1992.

———. *Praying with Power*. Ventura, CA: Regal Books, 1997.

Wright, Alan D. *Lover of My Soul*. Sisters, OR: Multnomah Publishers, 1998.

# Notes

## Introduction: Deeper Life

1. Chuck Moore, sent by email, May 6, 2007.

## Chapter 1: Intimacy, More Than a Beginning

1. Frederick Buechner, *Telling the Truth* (New York, NY: Harper Collins, 1977), 80.

## Chapter 2: Becoming Real

1. Richard Selzer, *Mortal Lessons* (Orlando, FL: Harcourt Inc., 1996), 33.

## Chapter 3: Intimacy Killers

1. Craig Brian Larson, Editor, *Illustrations for Preaching & Teaching* (Grand Rapids, MI: Baker Books, 1993), 82.

2. Elizabeth Alves, *Becoming a Prayer Warrior* (Ventura, CA: Regal Books, 1998), 53.

3. This quote by Max Lucado is taken from a greeting card.

## Chapter 4: Seasons of Intimacy

1. David Morris, *A Lifestyle of Worship* (Ventura, CA: Regal Books, 1998), 100, adapted.

## Chapter 5: Legacy of Mentors

1. Tim Elmore, "An Intimate Embrace With God (Part One): Your Intimacy With God Will Increase Your Influence for God," *The Leadership Link*, Sept. 2005, *www.growingleaders.com/index. php?id=81,199,0,0,1,0.*

2. Hannah Hurnard, *Hinds' Feet on High Places* (Shippensburg, PA: Destiny Image, 1993), 27.

3. G.B.F. Hallock, *Best Modern Illustrations* (New York: Harper and Brothers Publishers, 1935), 101.

## Chapter 6: Gifts for Developing Intimacy

1. Max Lucado, *In the Eye of the Storm* (Dallas, TX: Word Publishing, 1991), 11.

2. Craig Brian Larson, Editor, *Illustrations for Preaching & Teaching* (Grand Rapids, MI: Baker Books, 1993), 263.

3. Ibid., 9.

4. Source unknown.

## Chapter 7: Intimacy and the Practice of Prayer

1. Robert J. Morgan, *Then Sings My Soul* (Nashville, TN: Thomas Nelson, 2003), 131.

2. Dutch Sheets, *Watchman Prayer* (Ventura, CA: Regal Books, 2000), 153–155.

3. The Practice of the Presence of God, Brother Lawrence's Conversations and Letters, *www.practicegodspresence.com/brotherlawrence/ practicegodspresence08.html.*

4. Ibid.

## Chapter 9: Intimacy in Action

1. O. Henry, *The Gift of the Magi and Other Short Stories* (New York: Dover Publications, 1992), 5.

2. Hannah Whitall Smith, *The Christian's Secret of a Happy Life* (Old Tappan, NJ: Spire Books, 1975), 113–114, adapted.

3. Alice Gray, *Stories for the Heart*, "The Good Samaritan" by Tim Hansel (Sisters, OR: Multnomah, 1996), 87.

## Chapter 10: The Oneness of Intimacy

1. Tim Hansel, *Holy Sweat* (Nashville, TN: Word Publishing, 1987), 104–105.

2. Dutch Sheets, *Intercessory Prayer* (Ventura, CA: Regal Books, 1996), 28–29.

3. Walter B. Knight, Editor, "If—," *Knight's Master Book of New Illustrations* (Grand Rapids, MI: Wm. B. Eerdmans Publishing, 1956), 717–718.

## Chapter 11: Ten Virgins and Two Brides

1. Walter Lewis Wilson, *Wilson's Dictionary of Bible Types* (Grand Rapids, MI: Wm. B. Eerdmans Publishing, 1957), 334–335.

2. Ibid.

3. Melvin J. Steinbron, *The Lay-Driven Church* (Ventura, CA: Regal Books, 1997), 162–163.

# ABOUT THE AUTHOR

Alice Smith is an internationally known conference speaker and bestselling author of five books, including *Beyond the Veil* and with her husband, Eddie, *Spiritual Housecleaning*. Alice earned her Doctorate of Ministry from Wagner Leadership Institute in Colorado Springs, Colorado. She is a regular contributor to magazines, including *Charisma, Ministries Today,* and *Pray!* and makes guest appearances on *The 700 Club, TBN,* and *This is Your Day.* Alice and her husband founded the U.S. Prayer Center in 1990. Alice and Eddie make their home in Houston, Texas.

# How to Contact Alice Smith

Author, speaker, and preacher Alice Smith, and her husband, Eddie, travel worldwide to teach on various themes related to prayer, personal freedom, city strategies, and discipleship. For information about hosting Alice for a conference in your church, city, or nation, submit your online invitation at: *www.usprayercenter.org*.

**Prayer Resources**

Alice and Eddie Smith's books and materials, as well as other resources they recommend, can be found at: *www.prayerbookstore.com*.

To enroll in the free 52-week online School of Prayer subscribe at: *www.teachmetopray.com*.

*Free* **Newsletter**

Join thousands worldwide in receiving the Insight newsletter, Alice and Eddie's informative email publication. Subscribe at: *www.usprayercenter.org*.

To receive the Smiths' monthly "Teach Me to Pray" newsletter, write to:

Alice Smith
U.S. PRAYER CENTER
7710-T Cherry Park Dr., Ste. 224
Houston, TX 77095
Phone: 713-466-4009  FAX: 713-466-5633
Toll-free in U.S.: 1-800-569-4825
Email: usprayercenter@cs.com
Web site: *www.usprayercenter.org*
Resource Center: *www.prayerbookstore.com*

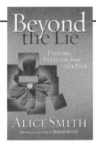

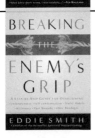